treasures of darkness

VOLUME II
"ECHOES OF A FATHER"

JOSEPH C. STURGEON II

PUBLISHED BY SERAPH CREATIVE

Published by Seraph Creative in 2016

United States / United Kingdom / South Africa / Australia

www.seraphcreative.org

Typesetting & Layout by Feline

www.felinegraphics.com

ISBN 978-0-9944335-3-4

DEDICATION

To the fathers and close friends in my life on both sides of the veil.
Your importance in my heart cannot be overstated.

Contents

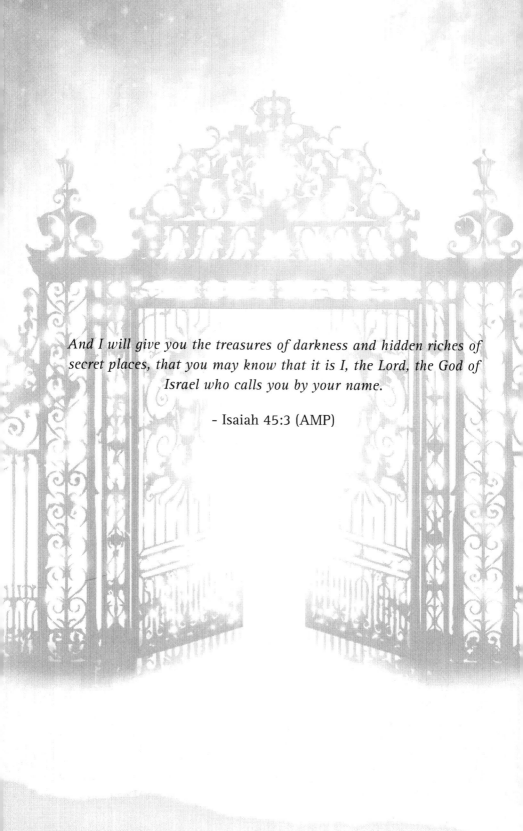

And I will give you the treasures of darkness and hidden riches of secret places, that you may know that it is I, the Lord, the God of Israel who calls you by your name.

- Isaiah 45:3 (AMP)

Introduction

I want to share a heart journey with you. Put your seatbelt on! It started one day while I was in college and working as a secretary of a neonatal intensive care unit at a very large hospital. It remains today the most intense job I have ever done. On this particular day, it was time for lunch and I was craving delicious nachos. I went to a local place I frequented at that time and sat down to eat. After my delicious nachos arrived, I looked over towards the entrance of the establishment and a man I had never seen before walked in. He appeared to be African-American, homeless, confident and at peace. As soon as he walked through the door he looked at me, walked towards me, sat down at my table and looked as though he had been searching for me. He had AMAZING blue eyes that were filled with peace and resolve. His external appearance was different than his internal world. At this point in my life I was young both in age and in the Lord and this was a first. Inside I was running over the possible scenarios, all positive. My internal conclusion was that I should try and witness to him but I did not know how. After about a minute of staring at the guy, neither of us saying a word, I began to feel awkward and offered him my food. He indicated that he was not hungry but did not use words. Instead, he used hand motions and proceeded to get out a pencil and piece of paper. He wrote, "My name is Edward and I belong to God. He is risen. Will you pray for me?"

I nodded in agreement and, as I reached my hand to take his, he grabbed my forearm like William Wallace. Smiling I bowed my head the best I knew how and attempted to pray. It did not work. I could not pray. In those days I was fairly good at making up a religious one and even that was impossible in this moment. The only thing I could think was, "Thank God this guy is deaf and his head is bowed." After a few minutes of genuinely listening for the Lord and attempting to pray I gave up, squeezed his arm to let him know I was done and said, "Amen." I could not eat any more so we both stood up and walked out the door. He took a left and started walking down the street where he came from. After he got past the window where no one could see him he turned around to face me. I was not prepared for what happened next. This man with whom I had just sat and had dinner with - the man who had a physical body and had written with a wooden pencil on an ordinary piece of paper with real words, who shared his name given to him by his parents - waved, winked and disappeared from plain sight.

Walking back into work was a bit difficult but I was able to manage and finish the day well. Later into the evening I fell asleep peacefully and had a vivid, transformational dream and encounter. I was standing in outer space when I saw Edward in the distance walking towards me - just as he was when we were at the restaurant. When he came within about thirty feet (10 meters) of me he transformed into something I had never seen before. From around him a glorified body came and enveloped him showing who he truly was. He was now in a glorified, brightly shining state dressed in white linen. This was a man in white linen, not an angel. Edward looked at me and said, "The entire encounter we had was not for you to pray for me, it was for me to see you and to trade into your life. That was why you could not pray."

The encounter you just read set me on a path to begin to learn about who the Men in White are and to have more encounters with Heaven. Here is another. It is my custom when I am by myself at home to pull out other chairs around the table and invite Heaven to come and sit at my table. This day was no different to any other nor did it feel special in any way, until my spiritual eyes were opened. Jesus, Peter, James and John appeared and sat in the seats I had pulled out. I saw them in the spirit out in front of me as clear as it would be if you and I were eating at the same table but in this instance they were not in physical bodies. Suddenly, my bagel bites did not matter anymore.

Jesus looked at me with with a genuine smile and said, "I want you to have fellowship with us. Now eat and we will all speak afterwards." Awestruck I watched as the four of them began to eat the fresh food that appeared in front of them in reflective silence. I could hear their thoughts as all things spiritual were available and manifest in front of us with complete ease and rest. They were reflecting on their life while on Earth and things that had just transpired with them in Heaven with gratitude and thankfulness. It was warming to see and hear their thoughts and watch them smile as they processed through them. Jesus handed me a piece of what they were eating which I supposed was manna, not having the foggiest clue what was about to happen. I ate the spiritual food and all of a sudden my natural body was no longer hungry. It was only desirous of more of Him. I contemplated my flesh actually being desirous of Him and realized King David felt the same way.

After about thirty minutes of watching this scene take place before me it appeared as though everyone had finished eating. Some finished before others and waited patiently but John was the last to finish. He knew he was loved and it did not bother him. He winked at me and I smiled. John was also the first to speak. He looked at Peter and began to talk to him of things to come in Heaven and on Earth that had to do with Peter's specific involvement. It seemed like a prophetic word but in this atmosphere everything was visible and known by everyone so it was not prophecy as I knew it. It was a dinner table conversation revolving around what Heaven was going to do and how Heaven was going to be involved in the Earth through the perspective of guys who knew everything about it and were going to be intimately involved with it. The honor and love I felt in being allowed to sit and be a part of this conversation was humbling and overwhelming. The love felt like waves washing over me and the honor was strengthening to my very core.

This book was born from the vision and encounter you just read and from fellowship with other "Men in White Linen." After the encounter I began to understand fellowship with Jesus and with those who had gone before me in a different manner and it caused hunger for change and increase in this direction. These men and women are ALIVE IN CHRIST and I had been given access. At this point in my life I did not know anyone personally who had engaged this sort of thing which made it all the more exciting. I purposed in my heart to go for it!

This book was written in a completely different way to my last book, "Chronicles of a Seer". One night as I was engaging Moses, Daniel appeared. They invited me into the Court of the Men in White to receive the scroll for this book. After I received the scroll and realized what this book was going to be about I saw that it could not be written in the same manner as the last one. This book had to be seen and written from a perspective of "the end from the beginning" and "the beginning from the end" in Heaven. While I had seen from this perspective before I was not aware of how it was going to translate into my writing.

Daniel explained, "You are going to have to be able to hold the entire book in your hand or your heart and see a chapter and write it. Sometimes you will be writing in Chapter Two while in others you will be writing in Chapter Eleven. It does not mean three through ten have to be done. It means you will have to be able to see the whole thing at the same time which will necessarily mean you will have to be untied from the Earth, your prophetic gifts and from many other things. It will not be possible as long as you are bound to the Earth, sun, moon and stars. Throughout the book you will be engaging in a process where words like 'time' and 'tired' and 'sleep' have no meaning to you anymore. If you are going to write the book from here, you have to be here to do it and those words have no meaning."

He continued, "As you will see on the scroll, each chapter will be you interacting with a Man in White. There are twelve chapters and each chapter will be you interacting with one. You must choose which ones will be included as all desire to trade. When you choose the twelve they will form a counsel for you in writing the book and they will be your advisors. You will have access at all times. Honor them as they desire to trade into the Earth and into the generations through your writing."

Undone I managed to ask, "How am I to choose?

Moses, who was standing by patiently answered, "Watch."

As I was looking a meeting was called among all of the Men in White. The bench of three (Heavenly government) was presiding and the purpose of the meeting was to decide who, where and what everyone present was going to be trading into. Once the meeting was finished I was given a scroll with every part of the meeting on it. It is with this scroll I chose who would be on the Counsel of this book. Their names are the chapter titles.

Once I chose the counselors, I sat with them individually and corporately to be advised and to speak about the book. At times there were things they would speak to me about that I had no understanding and had never heard. When that would happen I would have to go into darkness (yet unrevealed places) and find the answer to bring it into light so that it could have a place in my heart and in my day. I engaged early in the morning around sunrise with a cup of coffee when looking for something new to bring into my life. There is a gate between yet unrevealed places and light that I had to learn to stand in and administrate from.

This book took much less time to write than the first book. The first book, "Chronicles of a Seer", took four years. This book, "Echoes of a Father", took in total about six months to write. It is important to note that when I saw the book and all that was in it, the encounter provided a framework. MOST of the encounters written about in the book have happened over the last **eight** years. I put eight in bold to highlight the fact that what you are about to read, while it has been put together over the course of a short time, the revelation has been at work in my life for a long time. It is just that now I am able to begin to speak about it. I wrote the book as though it happened continuously so that the revelation could be released in a manner that allows the reader to come into the revelation, that took me eight years, in a short amount of time. You will notice some of the encounters are longer than others. This in no way reflects importance or any other aspect that may try and be read in to the book. I included short and long encounters for the purpose of the flow of the book.

Two factors played key roles in the amount of time it took to be able to write the book and articulate it correctly. Focus and desire. Many times it is hard to communicate what you see in Heaven, there just are not words to describe it. The only solution is to learn to spend all of your time there. Yes, I have a job. Several actually. I also have a family and friends. I am actually quite "normal." The key is through desire to learn to keep your focus trained above while you are functioning in life. As that happens your ability to communicate what you have seen from another realm will improve. It will not improve simply because you can articulate well as our Earthly languages are broken. It will improve because of what you have encountered beyond time and space. Beyond the governance of the sun, moon and stars where tomorrow and the beginning of time exist in the same place. That is where we must learn to communicate from. Even the words typed on a computer will carry a grace with them that has the ability to communicate far more than the feeble words can describe because of what you have encountered. That is the secret.

My purpose in writing this book (which was also my biggest challenge) is to open doors for others to walk through, specifically as it has to do with Men in White Linen and to represent the Men in White well. I desire to honor them. The book begins with a scriptural foundation for encountering Men in White as presented by Jehoshaphat and then moves into different aspects of what it can look like to encounter them. The Men in White have many things to communicate to the Church. I believe what you are about to read is a small part.

Lost in His gaze,

Joseph

Jehoshaphat

CHAPTER 1

"JEHOSHAPHAT"

AN EXPLANATION OF MEN IN WHITE

Sitting on a white sand beach looking over the Oceans of Eternity and watching the waves calmly lap on the beach I sat in awe of God and all He had done. With the sun quietly setting I looked at the multitudes of stars praising in the Heavens. In the Treasure of Silence I communed with the Father in perfect peace, all the while being infused with strength to accomplish in obedience. Looking over the Oceans I saw the people of God on Earth forming battle lines and preparing to war against the enemy. There were many warriors but few Fathers.

As I was watching the scene Jesus came up from behind me and sat down on the beach. Some of the men in the army began to realize that Fathers were needed and engagement with Heaven was needed in order to better organize and fight more effectively. Realizing they needed help some of the men fell on their faces and inquired of the Lord. As they fell on their faces they were immediately on the beach standing before Jesus. Before they could speak, Jesus - with a firm tone of one in command - said, "I will send you Jehoshaphat."

Pleased, the men disappeared and at the same time were standing up, hovering off of the ground in the distance. Intrigued, I asked the Lord what he meant. He said, "Listen."

As I listened there came a song and a sound from the distance, "O' when the saints, O' when the saints, O' when the saints go marchin' in."

Jesus looked at me with genuine love and said, "I must go now, but O' the adventure that awaits you."

Jesus then vanished leaving nothing but the wind gently blowing the sand around where He was sitting and an old looking scroll that appeared to have just been unsealed. It was the scroll for this book.

As I was examining it, the sound of someone walking towards me caught my attention. I looked up to see a man in white linen walking towards me at a relaxed pace. He was not very tall but had a peaceful look on his face so I stood up to greet him. He spoke with an elegant voice, "Hello, I am Jehoshaphat. I will be with you for the first part of this journey. I want to go with you and explain a few things to you so that you may understand and learn to co-labor with those who have gone before you. We have much to sow into the lives of the ones who are walking with God in the Earth now and it is imperative that you learn."

Excited and totally at rest I agreed and asked him where I should start. He smiled and said, "Take the scroll Jesus left and eat it."

I remembered on the last journey how the scroll of Isaiah fit in my mouth even though it was large, so I opened wide and swallowed it whole. I chuckled on the inside remembering how totally amazing, completely awkward and mind blowing it was the first time. Looking at my new friend again, wondering what was going to happen next, he explained, "What you know as 'the Men in White Linen' or the 'Cloud of Witnesses' have been around since before the days of Abraham. When Abraham sat in the gate of his tent and saw them, he was in the spirit just as John was in the book of Revelation. He looked up and saw them coming. While there was interaction before this, you need to understand that interaction has been written about for a very long time. Abraham interacted with them and the Father, and he had a working relationship with the Men in White during his day. Abraham is part of the Cloud of Witnesses and sows or trades into the lives of people on the Earth now."

Intrigued I asked, "This is awesome. Are there any more people who were written about that encountered Men in White?"

With a genuine look of a loving father he answered, "You have read about it, you just did not put the puzzle together. There are MANY accounts of this happening through history but there are a few you have read and may not have realized you were reading. Jehoshaphat quoted again the passage where Abraham met the three Men in White and said, "Abraham saw three MEN. Not three angels and not Jesus. They ate food with him as men would."

He continued, "In Ezekiel Chapter Ten, Ezekiel spoke to the MAN clothed with LINEN and the man in linen gave him instructions as to what should happen next. In Daniel Chapter Twelve a man in white linen is mentioned multiple times. In the New Testament, in Matthew Chapter Seventeen and Mark Chapter Nine, Jesus himself encountered, had fellowship and spoke with Moses and Elijah who were dressed in white. In Mark Chapter Sixteen two men were sitting and clothed in a long white garment and in Acts Chapter One, two Men in White appeared. These are just a few examples in the Bible. There have been many, many accounts throughout history where people have encountered those of us who are in the Cloud of Witnesses."

As he spoke it was as though new realms of information and possibility were opening up around me. Illumination and realization were being fused in me at a level I had never imagined, and from a place of thankfulness and great gratitude I continued asking questions.

I said, "This is so amazing to be able to speak with you. Would you mind if I asked a few more questions?"

"I will gladly answer them, I am sent here to do so," he remarked.

"Is what we are doing now considered necromancy?" I inquired.

Jehoshaphat burst into laughter, "Do I look dead?" Smiling I said, "Quite the opposite."

Jehoshaphat elaborated, "Those who have gone on are still alive in Christ. You are alive in Christ now and will be for eternity. Those who are not alive in Christ are dead whether they have physically died or not - but for those who are alive in Him they are in that condition whether they are here or there. So, no this is not necromancy. I am *fully alive.* The Church in the Earth and the Church in Heaven are one. We are ALL witnesses. The Church of the Firstborn. We co-labor with each other and we are alive in Him."

As he was speaking it was as if waves of information contained in light were being given to me. The wisdom of the Father to construct and imagine such a relationship was awe-inspiring. It was as if part of Jehoshaphat and the revelation he received during his life on Earth and in Heaven was being relayed to me in love. It was from "THE" Father but it was being communicated to me by "A" father.

Engulfed in Love and Presence I asked another question, "What is 'trading' and why is it you guys give and sow into our lives?

Without missing a beat Jehoshaphat replied, "It is one of our greatest honors to be able to trade and sow into the generation in the Earth right now. We are so excited, joy-filled and full of expectation for what the generation on the Earth right now will see, accomplish and govern. You are truly The Shining Ones. What is important to understand at this point is what it talks about in Hebrews Eleven and Twelve. First, you are surrounded by a Cloud of Witnesses who love you and cheer you on. Second, our work is not finished. What we have been called to do and the work of the Father in the Earth has to be completed. When we 'trade' or 'sow' we are releasing revelation we received or walked in during our lives in the Earth - and maybe a bit we received after - in order that individuals, cities, nations and beyond may fulfil the work of the Father destined and spoke about before the foundation of the Earth. In the midst of that process, what we were called to do and cause will be finished. The Church of the Firstborn is unified in purpose. Take this as an example: in Matthew Eleven, Jesus says of John the Baptist that he is Elijah who was to come. Elijah and John had a relationship and trading was a part of it.

"Part of the beauty of the pattern the Father has created is the cycle of revelation as it is sown in your life through us. One of the times where trading into your life is most prevalent is during worship and communion. A way to look at it is like this: as you are worshipping and communing in intimacy with The Father you begin a process where a place in your heart is being prepared *for* Him. As it happens we can see a safe landing platform to trade upon and we become the extension of the Father's arm into your life - completing the cycle. You receive the revelation through our lives and through our trading into your life. It launches you back into the same cycle of worship, communion, revelation and then transformation - where you literally changed from the inside out by the light and frequency of Heaven, of Love, of Presence and of Revelation - thrusting you deeper into the ultimate goal: being found *in* Him.

"The heart cry of your generation is intimacy. You refuse to be bound by the constrains of man and are not afraid to believe there is more to God than you grew up being taught. Now is the time for the lid to be taken off and we will all be there to help."

I was in awe of how much of my heart he understood and how much the Cloud of Witnesses were invested in our generation. It was as though an entire generation had been marked specifically by God to walk during this time. I became overwhelmed by the intricacies of The Father's plan and began to feel a swirling wind around me. I was being swept away by His Love and raptured by his embrace. The Father's ability to do something of this magnitude yet wrap me in His loving arms at the same time was breathtaking. Undone I lay face down on the sand and wept with joy for quite some time (hours - even days?). I did not care. I could not fathom the Father's love, yet it embraced me as if I was the only one who mattered.

After giving me ample time to collect myself and regain my composure, Jehoshaphat said, "Are you going to make it?"

Looking at my new friend again, appreciating his sense of humor and wondering what was going to happen next a gateway began to open in front of me. I peered at Jehoshaphat knowing he had a clue as to what was going on. Hearing my thoughts he said, "Scrolls turn into gateways. It is time for you to step through and meet Ezekiel. He is going to show you what the future involvement of the Men in White will look like. Before you go it is imperative you understand the importance of stewarding gates. There is 'standing in the gap' and 'standing in the gate'. Both have their place. When you stand in the gap you are asking Papa for something on someone else's behalf. When you stand in the gate you are assuming the role of a son as legislator and steward, administrating what you have already been given. Papa is raising sons who understand how to stand in the gate and administrate from Heaven what they have learned IN Heaven."

The gateway was made of pure light and seemed to exist in a place that was outside of time and space yet it was right in front of me. The gate had a hum that was so loud it sounded like a roar and was completely engulfed in love. Excited and unafraid I stepped through the gate.

CHAPTER 2

"EZEKIEL"

HOW MEN IN WHITE TRADE

Stepping through the gate I realized that, even though this was the "future" involvement of the Men in White, I was still in the eternal realm - so "what is to come" was as accessible as "now" and as what "was". This means it was plausible that what I was about to encounter could be happening now and could have been happening for a long time. It also meant that what I was about to see *is* a part of our amazing future.

Still a bit whacked from what just happened I took a moment to breathe and take in my new surroundings. I was somewhere above the atmosphere of the Earth looking into the Earth, yet still outside of time. Even though it could have seemed I was floating in space, I was not. I was not on the physical Earth. This realm or dimension had its own physicality. It was not the physicality that one would see while on Earth. It was a different dimension with a physicality of its own, occupying what would seem to the naked eye to be the same space. I was not in Heaven *per se*, but I was in a dimension higher than what we know as physical and I was not born into it. The understanding of being an "alien to this world" made complete sense. We are born of Heaven - from a very high dimension into a lower one. So, if we are not from a dimension but instead choose to go (which we did by an act of our free will while able to see our entire lives before we lived them) then we are "aliens to this world." This was also one of the greatest opportunities for us to be Christ-like - Jesus Christ coming to this world and humbling himself to be a servant in a dimension and world that He created, was the greatest act of humility ever done.

After coming into greater realization and illumination I looked up and saw Ezekiel walking towards me. Ezekiel was wild looking. His eyes were crazy like lightning and the frequency coming off of him was hard for me to manage as it was impacting me strongly. The way he carried himself was the embodiment of powerful, humble, gentle and as one not afraid of anything. He was free in everything he did, even to the way he moved as he walked with reckless abandon. Ezekiel, like many other Men in White, also felt like a father and appeared to be heavily involved in prayer with the saints. This knowledge of him, even though it was only a small part of who Ezekiel is, was discernible through the frequency, colors and glory ("wom wom wom") that was coming from him.

As he came closer I spoke first and said, "Ezekiel, I do not know a lot about you other than what I have just picked up and what was recorded about you in the bible that someone else has taught me, but I want to represent you well in my writing. Please help me."

He smiled and burst into laughter as if he knew something (or in this case lots of somethings) I was not aware of and did not answer or even address my request. I assumed he probably already knew more about me than I knew about myself and I was ok with it, so I did not consider it any longer.

With a loving smile on his face he continued softly but directly, "I want to show you a part of what the involvement of Men in White looks like. You have experienced much of it and that is why you are here, but we are at a time within time that people's awareness of our direct involvement in their personal lifestyle as well as cities, nations and even generations, is about to increase. As your awareness of what we are currently doing increases, so will the frequency and magnitude of our activity. The increase in frequency and magnitude will begin with trading but will continue into more that I want to show you now.

"The first thing I want to show you comes from the bible. Many have read it their entire lives and not understood. Most people of your day have relegated it to angels but it goes much deeper and explains an encounter you have had. Hebrews Thirteen talks about entertaining angels. The word and the reality there encompasses much more than most have considered. What the writer of Hebrews was trying to convey implied messengers, not just angels. The extent of what messengers can mean is far beyond what you now understand but you have tasted the beginning of what it means when you had dinner with Edward (written about in the introduction). Men in White Linen can be considered messengers. Now, let's go and have a look at how that appears."

Standing next to Ezekiel as he was speaking was like trying to stand on a floor that was vibrating a million times a second, except because we were in Heaven the vibration and frequency that came off of him hit me on the inside first. I knew if I was going to continue with Ezekiel I had to compose myself enough to at least hear and see what he was going to show me so that I could have a good grid to re-engage. Resolving to do so, I nodded at him to indicate I was ready to continue. Ezekiel reached out to grab my hands. Nervously, I grabbed his palms with mine and we were instantly in a different place.

We appeared in the living room of a house. Inside the living room was a man worshipping with great abandon. I will not go in to describing the man because I may meet him one day. As the man was worshipping Jesus, Ezekiel said, "Now watch."

Before a word came out of Ezekiel's mouth the light and the frequency and the vibration of light that was coming from him began to increase substantially. The light was pure white. It began to have physical effects on the man worshipping and he immediately lay face down on the ground worshipping Jesus. As he lay face down Ezekiel whispered something in his ear. The man began to weep and said, "I see you, thank you."

After about forty-five minutes, the man's awareness of the presence lifted and he stood up. He was so excited about what just happened he made a phone call to one of his friends, completely unaware we were standing there with him. The man's friend answered and he exclaimed, "Dude, you will never believe what just happened. I was worshipping Jesus and I saw my FIRST ANGEL!!! Yeah man, he was wearing a white robe and whispering sweet revelation about Jesus into my ear!!! Alright, just had to tell someone. Love ya, bye."

Laughing to myself and remembering when I had done similar things, I looked at Ezekiel with joy. He answered my thought, "I did not come here to be revealed or recognized. I do not care whether men think it was me or an angel. I saw a place in his heart for something I carry to rest so I came to trade into his life. It will cause him to draw closer to the Father. Mission accomplished. He will figure it out when it is time and he will be shown when he comes into a revelation of Men in White. Jehoshaphat explained why we trade into individual's lives, I just wanted you to see what it looks like most of the time. Until now. We are entering a new season and things are about to change."

"How so?" I said.

"Glad you asked. Follow me," he replied.

Ezekiel reached out his hands and asked me to grab them. I knew we were going to a different place. While I had traveled this way before, getting everywhere in this manner was quite different for me. I was used to walking or floating and taking in my surroundings but so far this journey had been more mission-oriented and it seemed more important, at least thus far, to gather information than it was to enjoy my surroundings. Ezekiel, hearing my thoughts once again said, "What is there to not enjoy about being able to move freely through space/time?"

Assuming the correct answer was "nothing" but having enough experience to answer correctly I said, "You can answer that better than me. Teach me."

He smiled and said, "Grab my hands."

I grabbed his hands and we were in a different place. It was another living room in another house but this time there were three or four people. They were worshipping with amazing freedom and abandonment. The glory and presence they were in while they were worshipping was overwhelmingly powerful. It was so powerful it was having an effect on me and I was coming from outside of time, visiting something that was either happening at this 'moment' or it was yet to happen. It brought a new understanding of Glory and Presence. It transcends time and space in the *now*. Smiling Ezekiel said, "Watch. This is one way Men in White will begin to engage and trade into your lives now. Go stand on the other side of the room. These who are here will together become aware of my presence and I will begin to teach and father them. If you are standing next to me they will see you."

As I walked around the men and women to the other side of the room I could not stop smiling. The Glory and presence became heavier and heavier as more time passed. Suddenly one of the women gasped and whispered to the others saying, "Ezekiel is standing over there."

The others in unison said, "I know."

They were all aware of his presence at the same time and saw him standing in the same place in the room clearly. Ezekiel addressed them all saying, "Hello, I am Ezekiel. You are the forerunners of something that will begin happening to the corporate Body of Christ. I am here to teach you. As we continue it will be necessary for you to keep your desire on the Father and keep your focus on me while we are together. In this process, one's distraction will hurt the whole group because we must move together. Desire to be one with Him is the highest form of desire and it is why you are being invited into what is about to happen. Keep your desire trained on becoming one with Him and what you are about to learn will change everything. There will be times when I or others will appear with you and the goal is for us to be able to go to Heaven and learn there together. Consistency will make it easier and it is up to you guys when it happens. This is just the beginning."

Watching this seemingly corporate imagination was great. It was a group of people who, according to Ezekiel, had set their desire on being one with the Father and because of that had been invited into one of the things He was doing next. They were to go together with a Man in White into mysteries and into Heaven seeing the same thing at the same time - and this was just the beginning. Ezekiel finished with the group and disappeared from their sight. Addressing me he said, "These guys are just a small part of who this will be happening to. What different groups of people will be taken into will be according to their destiny. You will hear of this happening all over the Earth and it is just the beginning. What will happen next you have already experienced in a small part."

Smiling at Ezekiel I asked if I could have a minute to process all that just happened. Before he answered I began to laugh realizing I could be aware of being outside of time yet still have a mindset that was governed by time. He agreed with a look which communicated I had as long as I needed, whatever that meant. Disengaging from Ezekiel and the group of people I turned my focus to meet my desire in the Father. In the instant they met I was engulfed in the same love and bliss that had whisked me away so many times before. Hijacked, I was beginning to enter realms of Love that could only lead one place. To Him.

In His presence I was complete and undone. Wrecked with love and remembering our last encounter, all I wanted to do was look at His face. Lion, ox, eagle and man. Changing effortlessly and with amazing grace yet with the power that created eternity, wrapped in love and infused with unlimited power He looked at me smiling as if I was the only one who mattered. Before he spoke I said, "I wanted to thank you for what you are showing me and I just want to look at your face for now if that is ok."

The absolute source of joy was overtaken with my request as He stared into my flame. I became lost in His face and wrecked with unspeakable ecstasy. It is difficult to measure time when you are outside of time but, after what must have been days of being lost gazing into His face, I began to be drawn into it. As I was being drawn in I heard Him say, "I am El Shaddai, the many-breasted God."

Trying to describe the mysteries and wonder I saw, as well as what was about to be released on the Earth, would take forever. The passage in John where he says all that Jesus did could not be contained in all the books, made sense. It was time for me to focus on something specific. It was hard because I was wrecked and overcome with the fact that now, not only did I have my desire, but I was wrapped by Him and moving in Him. Gazing into Him in this manner was the most wonderful thing that has ever happened to me. Focusing on His words, "I am El Shaddai, the many-breasted God," parts of who He is and what He desires for us began to come into focus.

As His desires came into focus I found myself seated on top of a mountain looking through time and space into the lives of some individuals. Their lives were as clear to me as my hand in front of my face. Papa was teaching many different people about food and being dependent on Him for it. What struck me as odd was not that He would provide food but that He *was* the food. He was not teaching them how to rest in the way we would think of sleep. He was actually teaching them that *no* sleep was required. The Father was not teaching people how to obtain things in a natural way, He was teaching them how to live from their **heart** and be **completely** dependent on Him. It was communion. In Him breathing air was not necessary and shelter was not needed. In Him time had no meaning and the need for affirmation was satisfied. He was their coping mechanism. He was their validation. He was their blessing. He was their source of knowledge. He was their motivation. He was their action and protection. Also, to these people this was not just a spiritual concept, it was their reality on Earth and in Heaven. Now.

Overwhelmed by presence, goodness and relationship, all I could do was weep. Being found *in* Him was beginning to be redefined in my life. Hours upon hours of incapacitating wonder mixed with joy and weeping enveloped me. My definition of what was possible and my definition of reality had been destroyed in a split second. I never imagined feeling so small would be so liberating. Wrecked, I began to feel like I wanted to come out of the encounter so I could get my bearings straight. As I exited the encounter and entered my body again my den was flooded with peace, stillness and glory. It was around sunrise, so I went into the kitchen to make some french press coffee. I love freshly roasted artisan coffee in the mornings. While the coffee was steeping I felt an even stronger presence come into the den behind me. I knew this encounter was not over but I still wanted coffee so I made two cups. One for me and one for the person or being that had just entered the room. I was not sure if Men in White or angelic beings liked coffee but I figured I would be polite and ask. When the coffee finished steeping I poured two cups, walked back in the den and sat on the couch next to Jesus. He had come in to 'my' realm.

After a long talk about personal matters He looked at me, smiled and said, "Watch this."

Jesus pointed his index finger to the ceiling and it turned to fire. He moved his hand in a large square around the ceiling and all of a sudden stairs whose source I could not see dropped down out of the ceiling. A large blue angelic being walked down the stairs followed by about twenty smaller ones. As they filled the room, small understandings about who they were came to me. The larger one was a teacher and the smaller ones were students. This was their first visit and they were coming to learn about humans who they were called to co-labor with. The teacher was a seasoned veteran and had many assignments through the ages but these Angels who were with the teacher had never spoken to a human or had interaction before. They had only learned in a "classroom." The teacher looked at me and asked, "Can they ask you some questions?"

Excited, I happily obliged. The first small one ('Number One') looked at me and asked, "What is electricity?"

Of all the questions Number One could have asked me I was happy he asked one so simple. Thinking I had a brilliant idea I looked at the lamp sitting next to me and said, "Do you see that light bulb and the light coming from it?"

Number One looked at me curiously and said, "No, I do not."

I was flabbergasted. Smiling I said, "Well then, I cannot help you and there is much you can teach me."

I asked if there were any more questions. A second small one ('Number Two') looked at me, smiled, pointed at a soda left over from the night before and asked, "Why do you drink poison?"

"I appreciate your directness," I replied. "I suppose I enjoy poison."

Jesus, who was still sitting next to me chuckled and Number Two seemed pleased with the answer. It was as honest as I knew how to be and the answer seemed to 'break the ice' in the room, at least for me. A third smaller one ('Number Three') piped up, "Why do people like fishing?"

I love fishing but I wanted to try and answer in a way I thought they would understand. I was one for two on good answers, so I said, "For food."

Number Three looked at me with a strange look. He had no grid for food! As I was about to begin to try and elaborate the teacher interrupted, "I believe I can explain. Those who fish for food and eat food in general have not *yet* learned to live and get their sustenance from the light and presence of the Father. There are a *few* who have chosen this path now and more will follow."

I latched on to the teachers words as if they were coming from the Father himself. The fact that the teacher used the word 'yet' was amazingly hopeful. If it was possible to do this with food then it had to be possible for all of the other things I had just seen. This process seemed like it would be a difficult one to learn but the intimacy and love it must require to begin to step into this place had to be worth it. It was so encouraging to be with Jesus and see that not only was complete dependency on the Father without the need for physical food, sleep and so on for the few but it was also for me. Captivated by love and awe I began to worship the Father again (my desire never changed) setting my focus back on where I left off with Ezekiel. In a breath I was back in his presence.

Smiling at me Ezekiel said, "Well done, now come with me."

Stepping towards him in faith we were immediately above a city I loved. In this moment looking at the city was a completely new experience. I could see the city but I could also see the scroll of destiny over the city, who in the city was helping it to be accomplished and how the trade was going to be put into effect and help the scroll come to pass. Ezekiel said, "I want to show you *a perspective* of what it looks like to trade into a city."

In the distance another man in white was walking gently towards me.

It was Moses. When he approached he smiled and said, "I have more to discuss later but for now watch as I trade Faith into this city."

Moses reached inside of himself and pulled out what appeared to be a ball of light and substance. Gazing at it intently he released it into the atmosphere over the city. Moses explained, "When we trade into a city, it is because we have found a landing place for what we want to trade. That landing place looks like people who have hearts who are prepared to receive it. Whether few or many, the whole city will benefit from the trade. All, saved or unsaved will have access to the benefits of this Faith landing on the hearts of the prepared and, while it may not land on some hearts, they will unknowingly reap the benefits. For many sons that will look like them being drawn into a deeper place of Love and Faith, using their current understanding as a hook taking them from the institutional church into the Kingdom. For others they will go deeper and higher into places they could never imagine because their mind is free enough to accept a reality they have not previously considered, and yet for others it will come as confidence to go forward into a business decision or investment. The scope of what this one trade of Faith landing on a city will look like is too broad for discussion like this. You must understand it and see it from a higher place your broken language cannot articulate."

Grateful and thankful I said, "Ok."

The instant I said "Ok" a beam of light which looked just like the ball of light Moses took out of his body shot from his body and hit me in the chest. I was astonished. When it landed on my chest I immediately began receiving understanding, emotions, frequency, vibrations, thoughts, his intentions, diagrams, grids and everything involved within the realm of trading into a city. Moses said, "This is how communication works and will be the way you and I communicate from now forward."

Excited and intrigued I asked, "How do I form one of those and shoot you with it?"

Smiling Moses said, "In Heaven, all forms of communication you can imagine, and some you cannot, begin with Love. Love sets the stage and, as it begins to manifest, creates pure light. It is the nature of a creative being to form Light then shape it into perfect and complete form through Desire. The Light is then delivered through Intention. Once the other person or being receives it, the frequency and vibration of Love inside them resonates with the perfectly formed Light, unpacking Desire and then they, through intention, act upon what was received. Love, Light, Desire and Intention are the four-fold pattern of communication in Heaven."

I was overcome with enlightenment and joy. As I thanked Moses he disappeared. I turned to Ezekiel, he was smiling. Even in his smile he was powerful. Being around him was like sticking your finger in a bolt of lightning. It was impossible not to shake. The intensity and magnitude of the Presence of God and the Revelation was so strong it was hard to remain in the encounter. I had to remain conscious and aware enough to continue even though there was a strong desire to exit and 'collect myself.' I looked at Ezekiel, he smiled and said, "Now I want you to meet Jacob."

Excited about what was coming next I rested deeper in the presence. As I progressed deeper and deeper there was a faint sound in the background. It seemed to be getting louder and louder. It was the Hallelujah chorus. Realizing it was probably not a part of trading into the next generation I disengaged and came out of the encounter to find my cell phone ringing. The screen read "Mom Calling." I laughed and spoke with her for a while, excited for a break but also excited to re-engage.

CHAPTER 3

"JACOB"

FATHERING FROM HEAVEN

Breathing deeply I was once again engaged, seated and back on the beach. Resting into the new encounter I took a deep breath, held it and exhaled saying , "Thank You, Father."

Immediately, it was as if Joy came and sat on my head. What started as a small giggle progressed into uncontrollable belly-laughter. Wow, the Father's Love is big! Unexplainable Hope began to fill me as my inner-gates burst open with Light. The overshadowing of Papa's Love began to engulf me like a blanket that warms from within. Content to be in this place for eternity, I began to sing the names of God- "El Shaddai, El Elohim, Yod Hey Vav Hey" began to flow with adoration from my inmost parts. Shellacked in Joy, singing and loving, I chuckled on the inside. My worship sounds much better in Heaven. Continuing to sing I heard another male voice join mine. Opening one eye to peep, Jacob was sitting on the beach next to me. Closing my eye again we continued for a long, long time.

Our singing came to a close but Joy remained. Looking at Jacob with excitement I asked what was next. Smiling Jacob said, "I want to teach you the beginnings of what it looks like to father and lead someone from Heaven and some keys to lead in that direction. Feel free to ask questions. If you are not leading people to Heaven you are leading them to yourself and these keys must become engrafted within you before you even consider talking to others about them."

Contemplative and reflecting I asked him to continue. He said, "The first Key I want to speak with you about as it has to do with leading and fathering from Heaven is 'dependence on God.' Sons in the Earth are still coming into this revelation but if you are to mature you must learn complete dependence on Him. He is the answer to every question. He is the source of all life. Let's look at resources. Joyfully coming into the realization and knowledge of the far-reaching implication that ALL of Heaven's resources are available for you and for what is written on your scroll, will annihilate any trace of doubt and any trace of a poverty mindset. At the same time, dependence on God as a key to fathering people from Heaven is not as much about eliminating negatives as it is about pursuing Him. So, instead of trying to eliminate negatives like doubt and poverty from your life, pursue Him first as your source for all resources and in doing so the realization and knowledge described above will be opened to you.

"He is the source of life. For every situation you encounter on the Earth there is a Heavenly reality you can exchange. Walking into that reality for yourself and understanding it in your Heart will drive you towards complete dependence on Him. I say it includes all situations on purpose. You see positive and negative situations because there is still a grid within you that loves the Tree of Knowledge of Good and Evil. When the grid is eliminated you will only see His goodness and, when you begin to see His goodness in every situation, Heaven's reality will begin to manifest in your physical life. Papa's Goodness is part of His nature and becoming dependent on His nature is the beginning of walking in all that was spoken about you before the foundation of the Earth - because you are escorting something that can only be learned IN Heaven FROM Heaven INTO your life.

"The second Key I want to talk to you about is 'Access.' If you are going to learn things in Heaven you must learn the extent to which you have access. Most people will not pursue things without permission given to them by another (Earthly) man or woman. It's tragic but true. As you continue to grow and show others the way the most important realization they should have, beyond complete dependence on God, is the access they were given and continue to have through Jesus Christ, the door. The access you are able to describe can only be what you have realized, but it will continue to grow for eternity.

"The third Key I want to talk about is 'Practice.' There are several different situations that work well to teach others. As you learn and as you lead people from Heaven it is important to step through the veil and go yourself. You should not lead others until you have much experience, you will be responsible for their actions if you are the one bringing them.

"The first situation is when you speak from a place of revelation. You are actually speaking from a specific place in Heaven. It is important for you to be able to see beyond the veil, so that when the time comes for you to lead others you can lead them to the same place in Heaven where you received the revelation from. At that point the revelation can be directly assimilated by the people who are hearing, because their dependence and access is in God. They can see it for themselves.

"The second situation where practice works really well, is when there is an issue seemingly impossible to resolve. If there is a problem, you should lead people to Heaven for the answer so that in learning it they become more like the Father. The answer may seem like common sense for you but there is more. Do not get legalistic; if you have seen revelation from Heaven about the impossible situation then communicate it - but leading people to Heaven and taking them with you to find the solution will benefit them much more. The foundation for every answer you have or give should be either you leading them to Heaven to find it or communicating something you have received from the same place. The Father would prefer you to have Heaven's reality over common sense. The former will contradict the latter. Common or Heaven, your choice."

Smiling, I asked Jacob, "Since practice is a Key, will you take me to one or a few places that would help me and others during our journey?"

Laughing, Jacob said, "I knew you were going to ask me that and already had a place in mind. What you should understand is Heaven and your experience of it is multi-dimensional. So, someone else may be standing right next to you seeing the same thing but would describe it in a totally different way. Principally, it is the same, but if you were sitting at your house looking at the sky with a friend and you both described the sky, you would both describe different aspects of the same reality. It does not make your reality more real than your friend's but you would see different aspects and qualities of the same reality and describe them as you experienced them. It is the same with Heaven, so do not get caught up in your experience having to be the same as the guy next to you. Enjoy and learn from all perspectives."

I thanked Jacob for explaining. The way he described it made perfect sense to me. It was confusing to me before why two people whom I trust would describe the same thing completely different. I wondered who was right and now I understood that both of them were right. Hearing my thoughts Jacob elaborated, "Heaven is a concrete reality, different explanations of the same reality rooted in different dimensions will rarely be concrete. In principle they will be concrete, but because at this point in your walk they are filtered through prior experience and broken language it is important to engage and see for yourself."

Enlightened I asked Jacob to continue. He said, "Ready to practice?"

I felt like a small child on Christmas morning and exclaimed, "OF COURSE!!!"

Looking towards the already open gate, the scene going into it changed. The gate was still humming and vibrating with Love, but now bright light was proceeding from it. Standing and walking towards the gate I began to feel changes in my body. The closer I came to the gate, the more the vibrational frequency in and around me began to change to be like Love. The simple understanding of 'what you behold, you become' now had practical application. Even walking towards the gate and making a decision to do so I was engaging it and becoming what I was encountering. A gate vibrating with Love.

Walking though the gate with Jacob, we were instantly in a different place. We were in a room made of the substance of faith. From ceiling to floor it was all the substance. You could walk on the floor just like a concrete floor yet if you touched the walls it was gooey and transparent. Looking at the floor ahead it was also gooey and transparent until you were about to take a step. Right before you took the step, the atomic structure of the floor changed into what you imagined it would be. A hard floor. Looking up, Jacob smiled and said, "From this place, through the substance of faith, you can see the Father's perspective on any situation and circumstance you encounter on the Earth. Go ahead and try."

Keen to try, I began to engage a particular situation at work. Looking into the situation through the substance of faith in Heaven was unlike any experience thus far. I could see the beginning and the end of the situation as well as the outcome and options moving forward. Surprised, I asked Jacob, "I thought I would be able to see what the Father wanted from this place?"

Jacob replied, "You will be able to see the beginning and the end of the situation, the whole thing. But, your ability to see the Father's Heart in the situation will have to do with intimacy. You engaged the situation from this place with the intent of figuring out what to do, not with the intent of loving through the Father's

Heart and governing well. You can always see the outcome of the situation from this place but seeing the Father's Heart and desire will require intimacy with Him. Re-engage the situation with the intent to Love and Honor and see how the situation changes."

I did as he said and the situation changed dramatically from beginning to end. Confounded, I looked at Jacob. He continued, "Whatever you see from this place will be from the Father's perspective because you will see the beginning from the end and the end from the beginning of the situation. The other factor is that He sees your heart, too. The situation will begin and end in the exact manner you see it unless your heart changes. This place is not about getting answers, it is about your heart governing well through Love. Love moves beyond a spiritual gift bound to the Earth into realms of intimacy and Love with the Father in Heaven only explored by those who are willing."

"Willing to do what?" I asked.

Firm and resolute he answered, "Overcome."

Jacob's words were so powerful, the instant the words were spoken they touched a place in my heart that has never been accessed and literally lifted me off of my feet and knocked me back though the gate onto the beach. It was violent but gentle. Landing softly on the beach, feeling a new area of my heart worshipping, I was content to give in. With no desire other than to worship, I lay prostrate for months, raptured in bliss.

Purity

CHAPTER 4

"PURITY"

ENGAGING YOUR DNA

Looking from the beach over the Oceans of Eternity, once again watching the army of The Lord in the Earth, I could see change. The army was wiser and better equipped to go into battle, but there was something that needed to happen deep within. I did not know what it was, but I was confident in the goodness of the Lord. Gradually, I felt a smile walking towards me growing stronger. It was Jesus. The way He walked was full of grace. He was never in a hurry but He always had purpose. Even His steps were well thought-through. Arriving at my side He sat down next to me and took a deep breath. Releasing it, He was content to gaze into the Earth. "What do you see when you look at the Earth?" I inquired.

Smiling at me once again He said, "Dirt, but sometimes gold. Depends on what perspective I am looking from."

I was positive the statement was loaded, but He was smiling at me making me feel like a child who was loved so I did not inquire any more. Instead, I waited on Him to speak again. After a while He said, "I have someone I want to introduce you to. She assisted Noah in his day and will play a huge role in the Earth and in the army you have been looking at. Her name is Purity."

Instantaneously, she appeared in front of us. It startled me, so I looked at Jesus and said, "Did you just create her by speaking now or has she been here all along?"

He smiled and said, "Both. You two have a lot to catch up on, I will leave you to it. Love you!"

He vanished and I was left with Purity. She was angelic and stunning, the absolute embodiment of Purity. Before she could speak I said, "Can you show me what it means to overcome?"

She replied with gentleness and grace that cannot be expressed in words, "That is why I am here. You can hear others talk about overcoming as much as you want to, but until it becomes your experience and your encounter there will be no benefit. Others will receive rewards for bringing the revelation to the Earth and sharing with the body, but it cannot benefit you personally until you experience and change."

"Please continue," I said.

Continuing she said, "Ok, first I will talk to you about what it means to overcome, then I will show you what it looks like and how to do it."

Excited and ready I said, "Good plan!"

Purity smiled, "You have read in the Book of Revelation where the statement 'To him who overcomes' is made. There has been much confusion in the Body about what this statement means. Let's start with what it is not. To overcome at the level described has nothing to do with adversity. Is there amazing things that will happen when you overcome adversity? Yes, of course. But the overcoming described in these passages has nothing to do with adversity. To overcome at the level described above has nothing to do with keeping your Faith confession throughout your life - meaning holding on to what you say you have believed and not saying anything contrary. That is reserved for the Church that remains in the Earth, not the Church who has taken Her position in Heaven. It also has nothing to do with using spiritual gifts correctly. That is reserved for the same. It actually has nothing to do with your actions. Once again, reserved for The Church who remains in the Earth."

I observed my life internally and saw parts of my heart which believed all of what Purity said it had nothing to do with. Looking intently at her I asked, "So, what does it have to do with?"

Purity looked so deeply into my eyes it felt like she was looking through me yet embracing all I was at the same time. Lovingly she said, "It means that you must overcome your entire human record. Your DNA must be changed and transformed."

"What does that mean?" I asked.

Purity replied, "It means every part of your DNA that is still rooted in the Tree of Knowledge of Good and Evil must be redeemed. That means everything from covenants your ancestors made with demon gods and the stars, to traumatic events that your grandparents went through, to the need to breathe oxygen, to the language you speak, is encoded within your DNA and the Father wants to redeem it and change it to look like His. If some thing or someone has access to your DNA, they have something IN you. When they have something IN you, they can control you and you cannot control yourself. This is why Jesus said, ""I will not speak much more with you, for the ruler of the world is coming, and he has nothing IN ME" (John 14:30 KJV emphasis added). This is just the beginning, your ENTIRE human record must be changed - that is what it means to overcome."

Looking at Purity her expression changed from loving and explaining to loving and instructing. She said, "Now, I want to begin to explain and show you what it looks like for your DNA to be changed. It begins with communion. It is important when you take communion for you to be actively engaging this side of the veil. When you take communion you are effectively trading the reality of your human record, your body, your blood, your DNA, your water, everything about your human existence, for the reality of what was paid for and made accessible by the resurrection of Jesus Christ."

Astonished I said, "Can you show me what it looks like to have your DNA changed?"

"Yes," she replied. "Follow Me."

Standing up next to Purity, we walked towards the gate. Being with her was seemingly pulling veils off my eyes. I noticed the gate was at the edge where the sand met the water and even the sand was life-giving. Looking up at the galaxies above was awe-inspiring. The vastness of the Heavens was enough to get lost in awe and wonder. Before we stepped through the gate, I took a minute to thank the Lord for His goodness towards me. It was truly humbling. Stepping through the gate, I noticed there was more to see in the time between stepping through and arriving at the new destination. I chuckled within, realizing that eternity could exist in-between thoughts, which is how fast we traveled. To my surprise, when we got to the other side Jesus was waiting on us. Joy remained and increased as I saw the One I loved. I was so excited to look into His eyes once again. Without asking permission I hugged Him. It was worth it.

After a long embrace I stepped back and honored Him with my posture and attention. Tuning everything I was towards Him, I listened as He spoke, "Hey Joseph, so good to see you. I am always so excited. Thank you for coming. I am going to show you your DNA and Purity will take you into it. She is to bring about the fulfilment of some very important things. She was with Noah and was part of the reason it was said of him that he was 'flawless in his generation.' She helped him with his DNA. She will be there to assist the body in coming into the realization and fulfilment of what I said in Matthew 5:8, 'Blessed are the pure in heart, for they will see God.' Purity of heart is directly correlated with your DNA."

Reaching into me, Jesus pulled out a strand of my DNA that was curled as 'normal' and straightened it out. Smiling at Purity

He said, "Your turn."

Purity grabbed my hand and instantly we were inside my DNA looking at it closely. What we were observing is difficult to describe. My DNA was vibrating dimensionally. Different parts of the DNA had different vibrations and even different frequencies. There were parts of the DNA that vibrated and emitted frequencies that were in a deeper and higher place than other parts of my DNA, and while they existed in the same space, some parts of my DNA functioned better than others. Parts of my DNA appeared to be 'redeemed' while others had things wrong with them. Nestled on top as well as within my DNA were black spots and other 'deformities'. The black spots were obviously parts of the unredeemed areas. I decided to choose one. As I began to gaze into it understanding began to flood me. This particular black spot represented 'fear of failure' and within the black spot there were layers that represented a generation. In this specific one I could see five layers, meaning five generations ago this particular vibration entered my blood line through a specific event and within each layer there was a generation that embraced the negativity which was initially created within our DNA. Also within each layer, there was a specific memory attached to the vibration where the person had a choice to either destroy it or embrace it and pass it to the next generation. With every generation the vibration became stronger and stronger.

Looking at Purity I said, "Let's destroy this thing."

Smiling she replied, "Its my Joy to help."

When she said Joy I got whacked again. Joy remained with us. Purity elaborated, "As you begin to engage Heaven to deal with your DNA there is something to remember. The first thing to remember is that no matter how much you experience, you always enter as a child willing to learn. There are protocols and how things are done is very specific, but those are for each person to learn organically as they grow. Approaching as a child until you mature is the way to go about it. It will not benefit you to try and do things the way someone else has described until it has been engrafted into your heart. It would be beneficial for you to look into the memories and events so that you can see what it was in your generational line that caused this to happen. Understanding is powerful."

I looked into my family line and saw the events and memories that were passed down. "Now what?" I asked.

Purity continued, "Now, knowing what has been done within the bounds of your family line, it is important for you to begin taking responsibility for what your ancestors have done as well as anything you have done. In this case it is allowing the fear of failure to remain.

Each one had a choice and chose to allow it to remain. Next you must understand that since you are a son you are underneath the covering of Grace. If you leave Grace out of this process and become legalistic you will not benefit. So, since you are underneath the covering of grace and you have taken responsibility for the actions, vibrations and frequency that have been allowed in your DNA, ask the Father to judge it and send his frequency and vibration of Love into your DNA. Once it has been judged in you and it no longer has a hold in you, ask the Father to judge everything in your life that is around you with the same fury and violence. It does not have to be complicated and as you come as a child you will learn MUCH more. Begin there and allow Love to show you the way. There are many things you will see, but the most important thing is to remain a child. Better to be a novice in the new than an expert in the old."

I now had a much clearer understanding of 'The sins of the Fathers being passed down generationally,' as well as one of the things that was being accomplished when Daniel asked for forgiveness from the 'sins of his fathers.' It was also exciting to put this new understanding within the context of the price Jesus paid, understanding that the price has been paid for our full redemption. It is for us to access it and appropriate it by Faith. Now we have a better picture and clearer understanding of how it looks and works.

Excited to go forward I did exactly as she instructed. When I asked the Father to judge my DNA, it was as if lightning began to bubble up from the inside. The frequency and vibration of Love was not coming from without but from within. It annihilated every aspect of the fear of failure and filled the hole from inside out. When it was finished there was no residue of the old sound and the freshly healed DNA was humming the sound of Love, just like the rest of the healed DNA. Grinning from ear to ear Purity said, "Well done."

As she spoke we moved out of the DNA and were with Jesus in a courtroom setting. Curious, I asked, "Did all of this happen here?"

Jesus responded, "Yes, but Faith is what mattered at this point. You needed to see what it was like for your DNA to be healed."

Thanking Him, I knew it was time to step back through the gate onto the beach. Before I stepped I took one last glance at Jesus. The wonder that surrounded Him was breathtaking and I could not get enough. Being in His presence was the definition of being fully loved and it was all-consuming. He is the only one who could ever fulfil that desire. I stepped back through the gate onto the beach with a bit more understanding and a lot more Love.

King David

CHAPTER 5

"KING DAVID"

OPERATING FROM REST

Standing on the beach next to the gate I began to look closer to see if I could spot anything new. My desire was to learn more about the gate and how it functioned. The gateway was opened when I ate the scroll but that did not tell me much. I had questions. Stepping back from the gate to look at it from a different view I could feel the Spirit of the Fear of the Lord coming upon me from the gate. As I was engaging with it and entering into the Spirit of the Fear of the Lord, I was startled. I could feel it coming from a different direction. Turning around quickly I looked up and someone I had seen before was walking towards me. It was King David. The Spirit of the Fear of the Lord was surrounding him. Stopping within a few feet of me he said, "Right now we are above in the Heavens. Your obedience in eating the scroll has created this gate and through desire for intimacy you pass through it. Once you are finished writing and the revelation presented is engrafted in you, this gate and this place will be shut down and destroyed. When that happens it will be good, because at that time you will have access to the revelation and the Men in White from within. You have no need to go anywhere, omniscience and every gate you will ever need is within. Allow the Father to take you to any others."

At the time King David spoke to me about the gate, I had not heard anyone speak about it in the manner he chose. Only recently have I heard others mention it. Looking at the gate with a new understanding of what was happening, I could now see one word written above it: Hope. When I saw it, I immediately understood the avenue by which all of what I was encountering would be engrafted in me. For me Hope was the key I did not have. By Faith, standing in front of the inward gate and repenting for everything in me whose Hope was not on and in Jesus, I would open the inward Hope gate that leads me to Love. In the midst of the Love through the inward Hope gate, by His goodness, Papa would begin to show me how to access the provision called "Men in White" who were to help me in the journey.

King David smiled, "What you have just realized is amazing and it will work. It is also an old way of thinking you need to begin to move from. You have not realized the most important key to move forward and it is actually causing you to try to move at opening an inward gate from the wrong direction."

Surprised I said, "That is good information, what am I missing?"

He replied, "Rest."

A long pause was taken and needed. First, to realize I had been going at it the wrong direction and second, because of the power his word carried. When he said 'rest' a sweeping, powerful calm and stillness came over me. It lasted for an extended time. When the power pause was complete King David continued, "Rest is the access point for reality. It is what allows you to grow in His nature and it is the beginning of responsibility and creativity. When accessing inner gates, as well as other ones, the starting point should be rest. When Jesus ascended he sat down at the right hand of the Father, indicating rest. Beginning to enter into rest is about allowing your spirit to govern the rest of your being. Physical rest is for the most part easy, the battle is for emotional rest. Your physical body will line up with whatever your emotions tell it to, so the quest is for emotional rest coming from allowing your spirit to govern. There is a Seat of Rest within you. You must allow Jesus to sit on that throne. When you give the throne up for Him to sit on he will invite you to sit on it with Him so that you can rule and reign together. Ruling and reigning with Christ also begins within. We are called to govern over galaxies and everything in them, it begins with governing yourself. The access you desire for galaxies will come from within. There may be external gates that are open for you in time but you MUST access the above from within. Many people, churches and communities of believers have been hurt and destroyed trying the opposite. Meekness begins with rest. Matthew 5:5 says,

Blessed are the meek, for they shall inherit the Earth (KJV).

Those who inherit the Earth will be the ones who have learned to operate from rest because rest is the beginning of meekness. Rest is the place where true strength exists and the place where true responsibility is bestowed. Inheriting the Earth is just the beginning. You have spent so much time DOING. It is time to learn to BE and govern from rest. This is training for Kingship. When you come at the Hope and Love gates from the direction you came it is about doing and performing. When you access Love from rest and allow it to show you what needs to be done to open the gates of Hope and Faith you are be-ing. That is what kings do. Kings 'be' through governing and administrating from rest. If you are governing as a King from Heaven you will have all of the information you need to make decisions. If at any point in your life you are trying to make a decision without all of the information, it is time to stop and enter rest so that you can see it from His perspective. Begin by surrendering the Seat of Rest in your heart again and continue from there. If you are not in rest you are being impulsive. Whether the decision you make ends up good or bad, when you make it out of impulsiveness it was the incorrect decision, because when you made it you were not joined with Christ. Impulsive decisions are made in yourself for yourself."

I thanked King David and he vanished. It seemed to me as though it was time to begin to engage rest. The thought of doing one more thing out of impulsiveness - trying to go the wrong way through a gate or pathway that was designed for my benefit - was sickening. I exited the encounter all together. I needed to begin to practice rest and I needed to begin to process everything.

My favorite way to process is on some sort of All Terrain Vehicle in the woods, or in a bass boat pushing it to its limit so I can get to the next fishing hole faster. At the time of my life when this happened, I had access to a Honda 420 Rancher ATV (a 4-wheel motor bike) in camo color and a gorgeous pond stocked with largemouth bass. I immediately grabbed my rod, reel, tackle box and flew to the pond on the ATV. This pond was a special place for me. It was a large, deep pond and surrounded by nature. Every time you looked around there was a tree shaking because of a squirrel jumping or a large deer walking. The water in the pond was always calm and, if you came in the mornings during the summer, the mist coming off of it was just about magical. Once the mist lifted you could look across the pond and see the reflection of the forest surrounding the pond. It was breathtaking, especially in the evenings. Add the fact that it was stocked with healthy bass and you had a recipe for seeing God in nature. I loved this place. Parking the ATV on the levy, I turned and looked across the pond as usual, sitting in silence (physical and emotional) for about thirty minutes. After thirty-five minutes, I began to feel a presence coming towards me. Usually this was a car going down the road, but this felt like a person. I started walking towards the road only to realize the presence was behind me. Turning around to look at the woods I saw King David walking towards me again. It was in the spirit but I was stunned he had come 'down here.'

Looking at him I said, "Beautiful place right?"

"Breathtaking," he said.

"Thank you so much for coming, why are you here?" I inquired.

"You are at rest here, I wanted to demonstrate to you that everything you access when you 'engage' is available to you when you are at rest. It is about being, not doing. Resolve in your heart to live your life at rest," he replied.

Feeling fun I asked, "So, now that you are here. How do you feel about my camo man mobile? It goes fast off-road."

With a mischievous smile he said, "Well, in my day we rode horses with chariots and swords, fighting with and against giants. I would call it amateur."

Belly laughter ensued. The fellowship we had after the conversation was nothing short of honoring and fun. While we joked with one another and learned about the differences between his time on Earth and mine, there was honor and life being exchanged between each other as we began to build relationship. I imagined he had a lot to say about worship and many other things, but that was for a different time. After catching a few fish it was time to go. King David vanished and I drove back home on my 'amateur-mobile'.

Arriving home it was time to work for a few hours so I got in my truck to drive to the next place I needed to be. At the time I was running a courier gig and was basically paid well to drive between hospitals. This part of the day was totally mine and I really enjoyed it even though it was gross at times. You cannot imagine what hospitals exchange. I picked up a cooler at location one and was headed to location two when my phone rang. On the other line was a broker who offered me a chance at A LOT of local business for courier runs. The man was professional and answered all of the questions I had, so I told him I would call him back in twenty-four hours. I was excited and the income was welcome. The instant I hung up I decided to administrate my work and my life in the way King David suggested.

Late the same evening as I was going to bed, I decided to surrender the decision as best as I knew how. I had more questions but I wanted to be at rest and begin to live my life from rest. My prayer was simple, "Jesus, I have no idea what to do and to be honest I am tired of thinking about it. Here I am and as I fall asleep I surrender and ascend into your presence."

This had been a practice of mine since I found out it was possible. I started dreaming vividly and lucidly in 2004 and it did not make sense to me why it could not happen every night.

Once it became a practice they turned from metaphoric dreams into real, vivid, amazing encounters during the night. Right before I went to sleep I felt myself drift out of my body into Heaven. In this encounter I was taken into the dimension of the business that had just made me an offer. I was taken into their computer systems. I was taken into their accounting system and shown how they make money and understood their margins and what their goals were. I am not an accountant and have no formal training in that arena, but I understood everything and even saw where they could make changes that would be beneficial for them. I was taken into boardrooms and allowed to hear meetings that happened in the past and meetings that were to happen in the future. I saw their visions, goals, how they treated employees and even the system by which employees would make suggestions. I saw the desire of the founders of the company and their motivations for creating it. Nothing on any level was hidden from my view. Even small quarrels between co-workers. Waking up the next morning was enlightening. My conscience was clear, so I asked the Holy Spirit why I was allowed to see. It did not affect me in any way, so I was curious. The Holy Spirit responded immediately, "We wanted you to have all of the information before you made a decision. You saw right and wrong. The purpose was not to sway you in any direction, the decision is yours. You needed to see what it looks like to surrender, govern and make decisions from rest."

I had no questions. The answer was clear and governing from Heaven was so much better than trying to analyze answers with partial information. The point of all of this and the decisions were not rooted in the knowledge of good and evil, this was the beginning of a great journey into rest and omniscience. Papa really knows everything and nothing is hidden from his view. I found out He desires for us to govern from the same place.

The Nazirite

Chapter 6

"The Nazirite"

Honor

Sitting in my glory chair (a normal chair in my house I use to engage Heaven), I decided to re-engage the beach. Before I closed my eyes I had a sense there would be someone waiting on me. Even from Earth I could begin to sense things about this person. He was massive in spirit. It would take a good deal of confidence and realization of identity to not be intimidated by whoever this person was. He was gentle but fierce, bold and brutally honest. Laughing to myself, I had enough of feeling what he was like and closed my eyes to go see him. Appearing on the beach to the left and some distance from the gate, I was immediately startled by the mountain of a man that was in front of me. He was a mountain not because of dimensional size, but of power and honor. Sampson was the embodiment of honor, humility, meekness and might - so much to the extent I considered bowing to show respect, and it was difficult to look at him. Looking at me directly, almost through my eyeballs into my soul, Sampson addressed me with a gentle tone, "Hello Joseph. I am honored to meet you."

Gathering the confidence to speak, still questioning myself, I said, "How is it you are honored to meet me? I do not want to play the false humility thing, I am genuinely curious."

Smiling he said, "You ask the question because you have no concept of honor."

I paused for a moment checking my heart, "Ok, will you teach me?"

Sampson did not answer my question directly but continued, "You must begin to see yourself as who you were before the foundation of the Earth. As you continue to grow in the knowledge of who you were then, you will begin to see the enormity of who you are now. Honor is first about how you see yourself, then about how you see others. Honor comes from the Heart and is the result of the work done within. Respect is the action that necessarily follows the work Honor has done in your heart. The reason you feel so much honor in Heaven is because the hearts have been purified.

"Meekness is the foundation from which honor grows. Strength bridled by rest (which is meekness) creates an atmosphere where honor can manifest. All of the men I killed were honored before their death not because of aggressiveness or skill or might (all of which were present) but because I lived in meekness. I had a sober view of myself (there were great areas of weakness in my life) so I was able to see those who were trying to kill me from the correct perspective and honor them well in their death. Because I could see myself well, I could see them well and was able to act accordingly."

Astonished Sampson could relate killing his enemies to honor in such a clear way, the only thing I could say was, "Wow."

Sampson continued, "Matthew 5:9 says,

Blessed are the peacemakers, for they shall be called sons of God (NKJV)

"So many in the body of Christ in your day associate being a peacemaker with either passiveness and non-confrontational rubbish or aggressive control. Those who conduct themselves in such a manner are the polar opposite of a true peacemaker."

Sampson paused and I asked the next logical question, "So what is a true peacemaker who is called a son?"

He continued, "To begin to walk in the revelation of peacemaking you must begin to lay the foundation of honor and meekness in your life. The three cannot exist apart. I made peace in my day, but it did not begin with killing an army. I was used as a judge because I had the foundations. The beauty of becoming a peacemaker is that when you have the foundations in your life, it can look however the Father wants it to. In my day it was killing an army of men."

"Are there any more foundations of peacemaking I should know?" I asked.

"Yes, as you grow in honor and meekness within the bounds of peacemaking, there is one more vital ingredient: Mercy. Matthew 5:7 says,

Blessed are the merciful, for they shall obtain mercy (NKJV)

"For many, mercy will be the hardest to grow in. The mercy of The Father is highly offensive for those who have not come into the realization of how much they have been given. In order to show mercy you must have the capacity to punish someone. You have been taught and the Earth works in a manner that when a wrong is done punishment is inevitable. The Father has the capacity and the right to punish everyone, yet He loved so well He made a way for the punishment to be avoided forever. He demonstrated mercy to the cosmos," Sampson replied.

I thanked Sampson for sharing with me and asked if there was anything else about honor he wanted to share. Sampson continued, "Giving and receiving honor both have to do with humility. If you are not coming from a place of humility when you give honor you are flattering in order to get something you want, like acceptance. In order to receive honor you must also be in a humble place. If you are in the correct position inwardly when you are honored, life will flow from both giver and receiver to the other person and both of you will be increased exponentially by just being in each other's presence. Honor from God works in the same manner. We must come to the place where we are so gripped with the Father's honor for us that we have no fear of the honor we give to others or the honor given to us. Papa finds us in the worst possible place, identifies with us there and shows us who we are and how He sees us - then bestows the highest honor of all the ages and dispensations and creations by calling us sons.

"He is able to do so because Jesus Christ took the most humble of positions on our behalf and demonstrated the peacemaking way of the Godhead to all of creation. The highest honor, from the lowest place, all the while knowing who He was and what He was capable of."

Trying to grasp the magnitude of all Sampson just said, I asked one more question, "Sampson, I am honored beyond what my words can describe. I am sorry to be slow, can you relate all of this together so I can begin to engage it again and wrap my being around it?"

Sampson smiled, "I am happy to help you. After I must go. I will put it in a way that is easy for you to grasp. Understand below every word are layers and layers that you must begin to work through in your life. It will be the joy of the Godhead to work through it with you as you will begin to grow in knowledge. True peacemaking is built on the foundation of honor, humility and mercy. All sons are called to be peacemakers and growing the revelation requires growth in the areas we talked about. Honor begins with seeing who you were before the foundation of the Earth and continues by having a correct view of how the Father sees you now. Humility will be birthed out of the correct view and is necessary for walking in Mercy. As you come into a realization of the mercy that has already been extended in your direction, you will be able to show others mercy through honor and humility, by becoming a peacemaker. Different people start at different places but the form holds and works together in perfect unison, drawing attention to the peacemaking act that shaped everything - the cross."

The weight of what Sampson said was too much. I collapsed. My realization of the magnitude of what Jesus did on the cross was just blown out of the sky. HE was the ultimate act of peacemaking. A sign in Heaven for all eternity of the riches and mercy of God played out through God Himself, who took on human form in the ultimate act of humility, showing honor to me; who would not walk the Earth for another 2000 years. The embodiment of mercy on my behalf. No wonder those who were peacemakers would be called sons. I could not take it any more. I tried to exit the encounter. As I exited all I could see was the cross. Every time I saw it I would get hijacked right back into the same weight and the same place. I resolved to stay there face down on the beach and be incapacitated on the Earth for as long as it took. Laying on the beach was all I could do.

After what seemed like years I began to become used to the weight and the glory I was being exposed to. Apparently it was not going away. Rolling over and looking into Heaven a wave passed over me again as I saw it - the cross on which the Lamb was slain before the foundation of the Earth, was in Heaven on display for all to see... forever.

CHAPTER 7

"MOSES"

FAITH AND JUSTICE

Moses was graceful, full of love and a bit freaky. I came to realize that the more my mind was open to Papa - and the more I desired and learned, accompanied by bringing myself into higher resonance and frequency through encountering Heaven - the more I was able to see who these Men in White truly were and what they carried. When I say "freaky", I mean I saw things that my mind said were not natural or normal. When you encounter something in front of you that your brain rejects as possible, you realize how much you do not know and how little control you have over the situation.

Compassion engulfed Moses as he walked towards me. He had an enormous, fiery presence that almost commanded honor and reminded me of the faces of the Father. Approaching, he smiled like a Father and stood next to me. I had longed for a relationship with Moses and had seen him trading into my life. This was the first meeting we had face to face. I was so excited about what he had to say and excited about spending time with him. Moses began, "Hey, wonderful to meet you face to face. I have traded much into you and into your generation. I would love to speak with you about a few things, but first I want to introduce you to someone."

After a few moments Moses continued, "I want to introduce you to Faith. Faith is the literal substance of God. When we speak of Faith as an entity or a being we are talking about the energetic substance of God manifested as a dimensional being. Because Faith is the literal substance of God, being dimensional in this case means Faith can manifest in any way it wants to. But the way

Faith manifests is always intentional and it will manifest in the best way possible to relate to you, so that you can learn and grow as much as possible because the Father loves you. Faith was with me all the days of my life on Earth. So, when you see Faith, I am not far away. Faith does a lot of things and will show you MANY amazing things, but it will always be directional. Faith will always lead you into Love, so if Faith shows you something amazing or teaches you to do something amazing, it will be by and for Love. Faith will lead you to give parts of yourself to the Father that you did not know were there. Faith will lead you to trade things you did not know needed to be traded, because the design of Faith is to lead you to the Father."

Moses paused for a second then continued, "I have longed to trade into your generation. First, because it is the Father's desire, but second, because the things I experienced on the Earth are for many to walk into. There will be no greater level of fulfilment in your life than to be walking in the things that were pre-destined and spoken about you before the foundation of the Earth. The Father loves you so much that He hand-crafted a journey for you to walk in, which path leads to a higher revelation of Him and a higher dimension of relationship with Him."

Watching Moses speak was breathtaking. He was not only communicating the will of the Father for my life and the lives of others but, because of where we were, you could see into his life - when he was on the Earth - speaking these words to those around Him, framing and creating the reality of generations to come. The words coming out of his mouth were so creative and so imaginative that they had not only the power to create a spiritual reality, but also a physical one. Moses had opened a path in his own life and had grown so close to the Father, that spiritual and/ or physical things he desired (because there was no separation of desire between he and the father) could be manifested openly in the physical realm right in front of him. It was just as easy for him to frame a spiritual reality that opened a door to walk through, as it was for him to speak a physical structure in place. It was seamless.

While I was coming into this realization, Faith appeared next to Moses. Faith was not as I had expected. I expected something very freaky but in this instance Faith appeared like what I knew as an angel. I knew from how Moses described Faith she was much more, but right now Faith actually appeared very simple, uncomplicated and approachable. I knew there was a lesson to be learned there, too. Moses allowed me ample time to absorb all I had just seen and continued, "One of the secrets that will allow you to begin walking in what you have seen, is humility. True humility is manifested in giving up control of your life. To walk every day knowing with all of your being that the full extent of the beginning and the end of all you own, desire and need, is Him, is the embodiment of humility and the beginning of power. Matthew 5:3 says,

'Blessed [spiritually prosperous, happy, to be admired] are the poor in spirit [those devoid of spiritual arrogance, those who regard themselves as insignificant], for theirs is the kingdom of Heaven [both now and forever]. (AMP)'"

Moses continued, "Many are under the false assumption that being poor in spirit has to do with poverty, weakness and false humility. Being poor in spirit has to do with humility and a sober view of yourself (see Romans 12:3). It is easy to see what you do not have. The hardest part of a sober view many struggle with, is to see what they have already been entrusted with. There are people who travel the Earth looking for a greater level or relationship with Papa, not realizing what they already have. They think their relationship with God should look like someone else's relationship with God, and that what they have will never be enough because they do not feel fulfilled. Their solution is within and they already have it. True humility is not defined as 'realizing what you do not have'. It begins with realizing what you do have and that you have it not because of what you have done, but because of who you are and the responsibility you have been given. Being insignificant has to do with not taking yourself too seriously. When you realize what I have said above, you will know there are situations where what you have been given will be needed - and you will be revealed. There will also be situations where it will not be needed. A sober view of yourself will help you determine the correct response. The promise linked to humility is The Kingdom of Heaven, its importance cannot be understated."

I thanked Moses for his words and looked at Faith wondering what the deeper lesson was in the appearance. Faith smiled and said, "Simplicity. While God is complex He is not complicated. He desires your love."

Moses continued and Faith remained, "If there was one thing that marked my life and one thing I would want anyone to see in my life while I was on the Earth, it would be love. Love was how I began, love was what sustained me when I was responsible for millions of people and love was what allowed me to consider them before I considered myself."

Moses paused for a minute. I asked, "There were millions of people and probably many more millions of issues. They tried to harm you, major injustice was committed and much wrong was done. How do you love someone so much that you would consider them before you consider yourself when they have wronged you and want you dead?"

Moses smiled from ear to ear, "I was hoping you would ask that question. One of my main purposes on the Earth today is to teach others to do what I did during my day. To engage the Faces of the Father and to sit at the Father's table. The answer is simple. The only way to begin to love someone who has wronged you and/or harmed you, is to eradicate the concept you have of right, wrong and justice through surrendering it to Heaven. The concepts you have and have learned are rooted in the Tree of Knowledge not the Tree of Life. Heaven's concept of justice and wrong-doing are much different than yours. Once again, even the concept of right and wrong through the Tree of Knowledge is rooted in your DNA. You must give up your right, and the ability in your heart to judge right from wrong, and execute justice from the grid you currently have and surrender it to Heaven and the Justice System of Heaven. This is why vengeance is His (See Romans 12:19-20) and it will aide you in having an unoffendable heart. It is not that there is no such thing as good/evil, right/wrong; it is that the source from which it is judged must change. It must be judged from Heaven - and you are the one who decides where it is done from in your life. So, to answer your question, I was able to love them because there was no place in my heart for the offense to land. I surrendered my right and ability to judge and took everything to Heaven asking for its counsel and pleading for mercy. I was able to forgive the people quickly, because they had no idea what they were doing. I could see, so it was my responsibility to handle it.

"I was immature in the beginning and literally spent all of my time taking everyone's issues to the Father trying to do it myself. While it was immaturity that caused me to do it, the act of practice in doing it was one of the main things that prepared me to step into the place of authority destined for me. It was preparation, because for me to take all of the issues for all of the people to Papa on their behalf and for the good of the nation (See Exodus 18), I had to love them. All of them. I had to love them more than I loved myself. It was preparation for me because in the practice of continually taking things to the court system of Heaven and receiving the knowledge of the Father on all matters, I began to learn His ways.

David wrote about it in Psalm 103:6-7 (AMP) where he said,

The Lord executes righteousness And justice for all the oppressed. He made known His ways [of righteousness and justice] to Moses, His acts to the children of Israel.

"David continued to speak about Papa's ways in the verses that follow. It is important for you to grasp these, because they begin to outline how the Father approaches righteousness and justice from Heaven and within the justice system of Heaven. Look at the next few verses:

The Lord is merciful and gracious,
Slow to anger and abounding in compassion and lovingkindness.

He will not always strive with us,
Nor will He keep His anger forever.

He has not dealt with us according to our sins [as we deserve],
Nor rewarded us [with punishment] according to our wickedness.

For as the Heavens are high above the Earth,
So great is His lovingkindness toward those who fear and
worship Him [with awe-filled respect and deepest reverence].

As far as the east is from the west,
So far has He removed our transgressions from us.

Just as a father loves his children,
So the Lord loves those who fear and worship Him [with awe-
filled respect and deepest reverence].

For He knows our [mortal] frame;
He remembers that we are [merely] dust.

"When The Father approaches justice towards any and all of His kids, this is the mindset He approaches with. So, if another son does you a great injustice, He will approach the situation with respect and reverence towards both of you. It does not mean there will not be consequences. It means Love will win. This directly contradicts the way most perceive justice, in that most men want justice so that they themselves will win, not Love. A great way to approach justice and injustice for anyone is by asking a question. How does Love win? This is what I learned during my time written about in Exodus 18. You must know His ways if you are to sit at His table."

Baffled, I said, "I understand a small part of the court system of Heaven and have experience there, but how do I get the Tree of Knowledge out of my DNA and grow in having an unoffendable heart?"

Smiling, Moses said, "The same way you do everything else, communion."

The realization hit me, "OF COURSE IT IS!" I laughingly exclaimed.

Laughing with me Moses said, "Off you go."

I went with Purity into my DNA and went through the same process. This time it was not a black spot but it was something that had the entirety of my DNA wrapped. It was dealt with in the same ease as before. After exiting the time with Purity and with genuine Love in my heart, I made extended eye contact with Moses, thanking him from the depths of my being. Moses smiled and disappeared.

John The Beloved

CHAPTER 8

"JOHN THE BELOVED"

THOSE WHO LOVE

Lying down on the beach looking into the galaxies, contemplating all of the recent encounters, my brain was totally fried. It seemed like so much information and revelation in such a short amount of time. I felt like I needed to be introverted for the next year so that I could process all of it, which was funny to me. With joy I thanked Jesus so I could make myself belly laugh. There is not a whole lot that beats brain-fried laughter with joy. It is actually the surrender of control.

While I was laughing a powerful wave of love came over me, which caused the laughter to lessen and an engulfing contentment with awe to consume me. Consumed by love that surpassed understanding, I took a deep breath in and out. Strangely, I could feel Love as an entity doing the same. In and out, in and out, breathing in unison together with me. After some time of experiencing this I looked up and John the Beloved was walking towards me. Other than the fact that he never died, he was different to the others in too many ways to describe, and he was the embodiment of Love. "Beloved" described him perfectly. The frequency of Love radiated off of him and from him. I sat up and then and stood up to address him. I thanked him for coming and asked him why he had come. Laughing, he said, "You're all about business, aren't you?"

Completely taken off guard, I said, "Wow, um, I do not know how to respond other than I guess I was purpose driven and not relational in that moment."

John the Beloved laughed with me, "Awesome, well, as you continue to spend more time with Men in White you will get to know us better and we can cultivate friendship. You have already begun that with a few of us. Care to sit on the sand, look into the Earth and talk?"

Honored and surprised I said, "Of course!"

He was so engaging the only thing I could feel was surprise. The Beloved asked heart questions and questions that really made me feel like he cared. I could not get over it. His questions were so good, but his intent was even better. There was no agenda, nothing except the true desire to get to know me. After thirty minutes of questions and answers and genuine, heart-to-heart conversation, I felt like it was a good time to ask him one.

"Can I ask you a question?" I asked.

"Of course you can, ask anything you want," The Beloved replied.

"Now that you have, for lack of a better word, graduated, what matters to you?" I asked.

Smiling, The Beloved replied, "I am so happy you asked. The answer is simple. Love."

Pausing to let what he said sink in, he continued, "Let me show you."

Putting his hand on my shoulder he said, "Look into the Earth and tell me what you see."

Looking into the Earth I understood I was looking from outside of time, so while some of these acts had happened many of these were 'still to come'. The first thing I saw was a person riding into a situation that was certain death. This martyr died horribly and willingly with immense love for those who martyred him. I looked at John and said, "I thought Jesus died so we could live."

He looked at me and said, "Everything you saw was completely pleasing and intimate to the Father. Your job is to fall in love with Him so much that it does not matter if you die or live and you trust Him with either. When you do that you will take a step towards not judging what you see by what you currently understand; you will look at this and see that no man has greater love than this. When a man dies for his brother, the greater love is towards the Father first because he has completely trusted Him with his life. It is from this greater love that the man was able to love the people in this village enough to die for them. Every person in the village will be saved as a result. He was a seed of Love that will sprout many Oaks of Righteousness."

He continued, "Look again, tell me what you see."

I looked again into the Earth. This time I looked into an orphanage. It was horrific. The level of starvation and hardship the children were facing was beyond words. Children who were barely two years old had learned to seat themselves at the table, put their own bib on and eat. In any other situation it would be remarkable, but in this situation it was because if they did not do it they would not eat. The person taking care of them hated them and since they were born the only things they knew were hatred and self-preservation. Many small children died in this place and it was acceptable because it was one less mouth to feed. I tried to pull away as tears were streaming down my face, but was encouraged by The Beloved to continue watching. As I watched the children seat themselves at the table I noticed a small, severely malnourished one leaning up against the wall whimper, unable to seat herself because there was a huge bruise on her leg and it hurt. The adults looked at her and laughed saying, "Guess there is nothing for you tonight."

They stepped over the child. I could not take it anymore. I stood up to walk away only to feel The Beloved step behind me and gently hold my face towards the Earth. He was holding me up and he was about to have to hold me back. "Take a deep breath and continue watching," he said.

After the small amount of food had been served, the adults left the room leaving ten to fifteen babies to themselves. The oldest was probably three. The children who were seated began to eat their food as if it was all they would ever get. I was not sure they were wrong. One of the children, still unable to talk, noticed the one on the floor whimpering. Without a thought the child climbed down off the chair and pulled his wooden bowl off the table, breaking it and scattering food everywhere. Separating the pieces of food from the wood, he gathered it into a pile and then motioned to the starving girl to come and share. When he realized she was in too much pain to move, the two-year-old boy scooted over to the two-year-old girl and fed her himself. When he finished feeding her, he ate what was left. As the boy finished, The Beloved let go of my face and I hit the ground. Undone forever.

Lying next to me on the ground, holding me like a father, The Beloved said, "This is a reality on the Earth. I would love to say all of these little ones will be rescued and live a normal life, but you know it is not true. Love matters and you just witnessed from The Father's perspective, feeling His emotions, one of the purest acts of unselfish Love on the Earth today. It is hard, but it is true, and it is an Earthly reflection of who Jesus is and the price He paid. Man may not rescue these children, but the pure Love they exude and demonstrate will be a testimony to the multiverse in the ages to come. The Father has a special place in His Heart for them and while they are alone, they will never know loneliness. While they may be abandoned, they will know acceptance. He holds them. He warms them. He swaddles them in Mercy and Abundance. He kisses them goodnight and plays with them in their dreams. While they may not see Him on the Earth, they know Him better than most. As children on Earth, their existence is grim, but the purity of their reality rests in Heaven and those children who make it through on Earth will have a lifetime of opportunity to step into Love that could shape history. You asked me what matters to me. This matters to me because it matters to Him."

Thanking him in a short tone I asked, "Can I just lie here for a minute? You do not have to hold me, in fact you can let go, I will be fine I just need to talk to Papa for a while."

"Of course," John replied in Love, "I will be right here when you are done."

"Can I be alone?" I asked.

"Certainly," he replied.

"I am upset and part of me is blaming it on you. I know you did not make me see it and you did not do it and all of that, I just need a minute to gather myself alone. Thank you for holding my head so I could see the end. Please forgive me," I said.

I looked to him for a response. The Beloved smiled, "You are loved and forgiven."

He disappeared. Taking a deep breath, I cried harder and longer than I ever had. I stopped involuntarily in intervals to catch my breath so I did not suffocate. I was devastated. Not knowing what statement to make or question to ask The Father, I closed my eyes and said, "Jesus, I need you."

The instant I called on Him I was in another place. Slowly, as I began to become aware of my surroundings, a gentle peace washed over me. I was calming down but still content to remain in the fetal position. I was on grass instead of sand now. As I lay on the grass, waves of peace washed over me slowly and consistently, breaking away the pain and heartache. The layers continued to be peeled off and I began to feel unmistakable worship, adoration and Love in the atmosphere. I knew I was in Heaven in His presence. After a significant rest, I sat up to find Jesus sitting close to me against a tree. Seeing Him brought comfort that cannot be described in words. He was so gentle and kind. Content to let me sit for as long as needed, He asked, "Can I show you something?"

Desiring to be around Him longer I said, "Of course."

"Take my hand," He instructed, reaching out His hand, "Matthew 5:4 says,

"Blessed are those who mourn, for they will be comforted (KJV)."

"It is important for you to know that Heaven's reality is the place from which you will receive true comfort and Holy Spirit is the One who will bring you into the reality. His name is Comforter because He leads you to Me and I am the embodiment of Heaven's reality. Heaven's reality should become your sole coping mechanism during hard times. When you trade your reality for Heaven's reality you are trading your life for Mine."

Grabbing His hand was the answer to all of my questions. He turned my weeping to Joy. Walking with Him on the grass was the most liberating and restoring moment I can remember. It was as if nothing mattered but He and I being together. Continuing to walk together, the atmosphere around us began to change from worship, adoration and Love to heightened joy and extreme laughter. The further we walked the heavier it got. The line between being able to walk and incapacitating belly laughter was growing thin and whatever was causing it was over the next hill. We arrived at the top of the hill and paused for a moment. Gazing down the other side was a moment I will never forget. My laughter turned to shouting, "YES!!! I KNEW IT!!!"

On the other side of the hill, just down below me, was the source of Joy and laughter I felt. Children, everywhere! Jesus smiled and laughed with tears of Joy, "Not one is forgotten. All of the children who came to the Earth and were rejected either through abortion or some other injustice, will have a place to grow up in Heaven. This place is special and set aside for them so that they can have the opportunity to grow and mature just like you do when you are in the Earth. They have only the best teachers and guardians who lived in the Earth. For now, they stay here in this area but only until they mature."

Smiling contagiously I thanked Jesus and hugged Him. Looking at me with Love He said, "I want to stay with you too, but for now it is important for you to begin and continue building relationship with Men in White Linen. You and others must come into a deeper revelation of the Church in Heaven and the Church on the Earth being one church. Relationship and co-laboring with them will be seamless sooner than you think. Like anything else it will be rejected before it becomes normal, just be patient. I love you."

Jesus smiled and I was transported back to the beach. John the Beloved was waiting on me with a big smile, "Broseph! So good to see you again. I know what you saw was hard to watch. I also knew it would be worth it. So many in the body of Christ avoid pain like the plague because it forces them to realize their own. Love is at its best in the midst of heartache. It does not mean there is no Love without pain. There is beautiful, intimate, amazing Love without pain, like a father looking into the eyes of his daughter for the first time or the intimate bond between mother and son. It means Love is expressed well in pain because there has been an acute realization of un-love. Love is selfless and a choice first, so its expression thrives in selfish environments of un-love. I want to show you one more selfless act of Love. Do you care to see it?"

Understanding everything The Beloved had just explained, I agreed. Putting his hand on my shoulder, he asked me to look into the Earth again. Looking into the Earth this time there was a different scene. This time as I looked I saw an enormous garbage dump. There were people who lived in the garbage dump. The words nasty and horrific do not begin to describe the conditions they lived under. This was a place where even teenagers either starved to death or were so sick they died. Looking closer at the dump I saw a specific child, no more than six years old, who had been left there because his parents could not take care of him. This was a child who had always known hunger and never known love. All of his days on the Earth he never felt love. He was dying and would probably make it a few more hours, but after that he would be gone. Understanding a little bit more about how Love works and thrives, unable to intervene in this situation, I was curious what would happen. While I was looking at the scene two people whom I would call 'missionaries', walked into the dump and found this child. Stepping aside to talk before they arrived in hearing distance of the child, the first missionary had great compassion. The second, who was still in a learning process said, "Leave him, he will not make it."

Filled with compassion for both the second missionary and the child, the first missionary looked at the second and said bluntly, "That is not the point!"

The second missionary replied, "I do not get it?"

The first missionary said, "I see that. Here is my heart. This child has never known love. All the days of his life he has never been loved. I want to hold him in my arms until he dies, because when he gets to Heaven I want his last memory of the Earth to be Love. He will not have pain when he gets there but he will have memory. Why can't the last one be of Love?"

Back on the beach with John the Beloved, I was undone again. Looking at me as the embodiment of compassion, John, the one who is loved, gazed at me with tears in his eyes, eternal acceptance and abounding care, saying, "Love matters."

CHAPTER 9

"ENOCH"

UNTIE FROM THE EARTH

I could not handle sitting and crying anymore, so I decided to go for a walk. Strolling down the shoreline of the beach, warm water softly hitting my feet, I could feel waves and waves of powerful energy begin to wash over me. With varying intensity the energy released a refreshing pleasantness into my being. Stopping to enjoy the moment, I gazed back into the Earth at the army that had been there since the beginning. My perspective of 'the army' began to change. They no longer looked like an army - in fact, they never were an army. "Army" was my Earth-bound perspective that was now completely overshadowed by Love for 'sons' and the desire to manifest the manifold faces of Papa in the Earth. Great joy came over me as I looked. The army as a whole had come into the same revelation and they could not continue any further in the work the Lord had pre-ordained for them on that side of the veil. They had to transition into rest. There was a marked hesitation in the 'sons', because they knew they had come to a place where the decision meant they would cross the point of no return. It was wisdom for those who were about to make this decision to consider all things. As I was watching the sons in the Earth contemplate the decision, I could feel enormous - almost incapacitating - grace and power walking up behind me. Turning around to look behind me, I saw something freaky and hard to describe. It was Enoch. The only way I was able to tell his identity this time was because I knew in my heart who it was and could not tell by outward appearance. He was the embodiment of Love, but he was flickering in and out of dimensions so fast it was hard to comprehend. Every now and again, when in Heaven you stand next to something or someone who is so much more powerful than you can comprehend, it is actually scary because you realize the extent to which you are not in control. This was one of those moments. Standing next to me, he took a deep breath and said, "I have so much invested in your generation and I am so excited about what lies ahead for all of us. It is truly a time like never seen before."

As Enoch was speaking some sons in the Earth began to make the decision to transition. They were instantly standing on the beach with us. When all those who made the decision had transitioned to the side of the veil we were on, we stood in a circle, Enoch with us. Enoch spoke first, "I want to teach you all about the transcendent life as well as untying from your human record. So, from now on I will not use words as you understand them. I will use light to communicate and you will need to unpack it yourself. Every conversation and every answer to all of your questions for now will be contained within. I am here to help. Ready?"

The people who had come did not seem as freaked out by Enoch as me and I remembered Heaven is multi-dimensional. Suddenly, a beam of light left Enoch's body, split in every direction needed and impacted us in the chest. Right when the others were impacted they returned to Earth and I was left with Enoch. I thought to myself, "Why communicate through a light beam and not speak?"

Enoch smiled and answered my thought-question with his thoughts, "To answer your question, I am speaking to you through thoughts and blasting people with light because you need to understand all that is available. One day soon all communication will be with light. Even while you are on Earth you can communicate like this. It is time for you to begin unpacking the light. You already know how to do it, so begin. It is time for more focus."

I thanked Enoch and he dimensioned away. Taking a deep breath, I turned my focus and desire towards the inward light I just received. I chuckled remembering Heaven lives inside and that full access was granted through Jesus. By faith, as I turned my focus and desire inward, I engaged the resonation of Love manifesting as light within that I received from Enoch. From within I gave it a hug and held it tight, allowing the resonation of Love that was already in me (as a result of coming into the realization that Jesus loved me first) to react with that which was received. The instant I began, the desires of the Father began to unpack within me, laying out what I could see were a series of conversations and revelations I was to have with Enoch about being untied from the Earth. These conversations and revelations for me were to be the beginning of the revelation of living a transcendent life and untying from the Earth and from my human record - just as Enoch said. There was no particular order of importance, but I could see all of them at once. I could also engage with all of them at once, however, since my brain was still a bit fried and I was still quite whacked, I decided to take them one at a time from left to right. As I engaged them I was back on the beach in the same place with Enoch. Confused I asked, "How is it that I am back here; I was engaging within and you just flickered out of sight right before I started? I feel like a puppy with its head turned sideways."

Enoch laughed out loud, "There are many paths to engage the Heavens and you just learned another. There are many paths but only one door you should go through. Jesus is the door you should go through, no other. Now, what we are about to speak of is the manifestation of what you are engaging within the light bubble that I gave you. I am speaking to you in this manner because this is the 'working out within you' and you need to see what it looks like. There will soon come a time where this is not necessary as you will be able to unpack, assimilate and act on the revelation through intention immediately. What we are about to speak about is not a formula. It only begins to reveal what it looks like to untie from the Earth and from your human record. Once you see this and what it looks like, you can engage on your own and it will begin to happen instantly.

"The first thing I want to talk to you about is actually untying from the frequency of the Earth. You have spoken with others before about being Earth-bound, so I want to elaborate on it a bit more. The Earth, as well as every other star and planet, emit a frequency and a sound. The frequency and sound of the Earth is in you, around you and it moves through you. It has been that way since the fall. You must first, by faith, break the frequency of the Earth that surrounds you and then move inward. You do not want any part of you to be Earth-bound - including your flesh. On the note of being Earth-bound, I want to talk to you about the purpose of pain. Pain is mysterious. When painful events happen in your life they can have one of two effects. The first effect pain can have is that it can powerfully bind you to the Earth. Some people experience so much that it takes years to overcome. The Father can use it as well. The other direction painful events in your life can take is that it can thrust you into resurrection momentum. It is your choice every time. As you continue to see and experience painful things in your life, you will come to know the "fellowship of His sufferings" and they will lead you to the "power of His resurrection" (Philippians 3:10). Few choose the latter, but the Father delights in taking things intended for your destruction and using them for your salvation and the salvation of others. Matthew 5:10 says,

"Blessed are they who are persecuted for righteousness sake, for theirs is the Kingdom of Heaven (KJV)."

"This is your invitation into the realization of all you have been given through choosing to use pain as a catalyst to thrust you into intimacy with the Father."

I tried to think of something smart to say but the only thing that came out was, "Wow."

Enoch continued, "Next, there are so many areas of people's lives where they believe something they received as a result of the fall, is how they were made and what they were made for. For example, there are conditions you developed over your lifetime that have nothing to do with how you were created. Look at introvertedness vs. extrovertedness. You were not created for either. You were created to Love. One receives energy so that it can love from being alone and the other receives energy so that it can love by being with others. Neither of those come from the Father. It is time to trade your introvertedness for His strength, so that you can Love well. This practice of trading your human condition for His Love will help you.

"The next thing I want to talk to you about is your gifts. There are so many people in the Earth whose identities are tied up in their gifts and not in sonship. When this age ends and the new one begins, the gifts you have been given will no longer be necessary and they will be taken away. What will you have left?"

I answered as honestly as I knew how, "I genuinely do not want to think about it, because the answer is probably not much."

Enoch replied, "You will have more than you think, but the point is that your relationship with the Father is based on heart matters, not gifts. It is based on Love and as long as your identity is wrapped up in your gifts you will not progress in relationship and character. I am not saying gifts are invalid and do not have a place. They do have a place with the Church in the Earth. What I am saying is that there comes a point in your walk where you must surrender them to move forward in Love and join the Church in Heaven, operating as a Son. There are no Prophets in Heaven. There are no spiritual gifts in Heaven. The question is all about your access point. Do you stand in the Earth and talk about what God is like, or do you come down from Heaven and bring it all with you? When you come from Heaven you do not talk about anything, you become everything you have been designed for and you terraform everything in your path."

The truth was so hard to accept it knocked me out of the encounter and I was back in my chair on Earth. My internal questions were a total distraction and most of them were not about me. I was accustomed to being in places where you were celebrated because of your gifts and it was a turnoff. I was really ready to give my gifts up - but how do you tell close friends and people you love who have invested thirty years in gifting (and even based their ministry around it) that there is a better way to go? A way which would require them to give everything up. They would lose all of it and I would lose friends. What about everything I have invested?

Suddenly Jesus appeared on the couch across from my chair. "Hi Joseph," He said.

"I'm confused," I replied.

He looked at me with a 'tough love' look and said in the same kind of tone, "Enoch told you that the gifts have their place; **they do**. All of your other questions are rooted in the fear of man and self-pity. We have better things to do and you are well-equipped to deal with it. Purity made a wise statement when she said, "Better to be a novice in the new than an expert in the old." There will only be a few who choose to move forward, but it is the same with most of the things done in the Earth. Many times the ones who caught the last thing resist the new thing. That's not your problem right now. Move forward and grow."

In moments like these I really appreciate His directness. It was not nice, it was the requirement of a bit more maturity. Niceness is powerlessness and Jesus has no issues there. He is kind beyond our wildest imagination, but He is not one to roll over being nice, making excuses for areas where we need change. I did not want to be babied; "tough" and "love" do fit in the same sentence.

"Thank you, what You said is relieving and my heart is well-prepared to move forward. So again, thank you," I said.

Jesus smiled and disappeared.

Excited, I re-engaged the light within and was back on the beach with Enoch. I told him I was ready to progress and he continued where he left off, "Trading your gifts is another function of trading things that bind you to the Earth. They too will pass away with this age.

The last thing I want to speak to you about will be the best and most freeing thing we have spoken about thus far. You have done well up to this point. One of the most profound things you can begin to trade is your revelation of your position. You are seated in Heaven. There is no need to pull things down from Heaven, you are actually supposed to be administrating what you have already been given. It is time to transition away from receiving of Heaven to becoming the quantum-energetic resource of Heaven. It is time to become the never-ending supply. As long as you are looking to receive something from Heaven you will never shift into being Heaven's resource to the Earth and you will be bound to the Earth because of it. It is time for you to trade the mindset of receiving things from God on the Earth. Trade every revelation you have ever received of Him and how He is on the Earth-side of the veil because it is Earth-bound. I am not asking you to trade your salvation. It is set; Jesus is the Way. What I am saying is whenever you receive something from Heaven, it must pass through your filter of what you already believe and know about Him. The time has come to lay down everything you learned about God while not on this side of the veil. Initially, growing in Him is about trading parts of your filter because of what happens to you. Eventually you have to destroy it and give up all revelation you received, beginning again like the Apostle Paul, knowing only Christ and Him crucified. We must be what we learn in Heaven, then we become Heaven's resource on Earth."

The power and authority with which Enoch spoke was wrecking. I opened my mouth to speak but no words came out. The thought and the honor bestowed upon someone to be invited to become Heaven's resource on Earth through what they learned from Him in Heaven was more than I could take - and it is extended to everyone. For the Body of Christ to individually be trusted by an all-powerful God, Whom had people like Enoch and the saints of old at His wish and command, to grow into a place where Heaven was the resource, was an honor I had no grasp for. I did not know whether to cry or kneel, so I did both and ended up in a ball on the sand with tears of joy and a love vibrating on the inside I still do not understand. I lay there in joy for a long, long time.

After I had time to collect myself, I sat up to find Enoch sitting next to me seated on the sand. He seemed very pleasant and pleased to sit in silence. We sat next to each other and enjoyed silence listening to the ocean for a while. When the appropriate amount of time had passed, I began to pray, "Father I love you. Thank you for your goodness and your mercy. Father, by faith I want to begin to trade and come into heart knowledge of these things and I need some help. So, help me please."

Enoch interrupted me, "Communion is a good place to start."

Smiling, I said, "Yep, that is what help looks like. Thanks. How do I do that on this side of the veil?"

Enoch replied, "Well, depends on your faith. You can go to the other side (Earth), get elements and bring them back here with you if you like. As soon as your elements hit the veil they will transform into the body and blood of Jesus. Your other option is to go to some of the many trading floors. Jesus' body and Jesus' blood are trading floors and there are many more. The last thing you can do is trade by faith wherever you are, including right here as long as you are trading on the body and blood of Jesus.

Everyone starts somewhere and, as you begin, your faith is more important than where and how you do it."

"Thank you," I said.

Focusing I continued, "Ok Papa. Thanks for your help. By faith I step onto the correct trading floors in the correct places. Jesus, I no longer desire to be tied to the Earth in any way so I ask that areas where I am bound to the Earth would be revealed to me. By faith I want to trade my gifts but first I want to be honest and vulnerable with You about them. At times I have used the gifts You have given me for my own gain and, at times, I have used the gifts you gave me in self-defense. I have used the gifts You gave me for self-promotion and have led people to myself instead of You. I do not think I did it maliciously, but there were times where I was aware that I was doing it for self-preservation and I did not care. It was void of character."

I began to weep and closed my eyes, "Jesus, facing this is part of the reason I did not want to give my gifts up. Yes, it was the fear of man but, if I were to be completely honest, I would say parts of my heart still do not believe You, the Father or anyone are good enough to forgive me. I have a hard time trusting You with those parts of my heart, even though I know You can see them. My head knows You're good, but not all of my heart does and those parts of my heart believe You love me based on my actions. I thought the black cloud* took care of it - but here we are. So, here I am. I am so sorry. I want to trade my gifts. I have chosen them over Love. Take them. I only ask for You in return. Whatever it takes."

Opening my tear-filled eyes on the beach, I felt the grace for gifts lift off of me like taking off a hooded jumper. Suddenly, I lost sixty percent of the clarity I had and everything was fuzzy. This clear, beautiful place I so enjoyed was now a confusing mess in my clouded eyes. To my horror, I realized much of my ability to see and engage with Heaven was not sonship but purely gifting - gifting that would be taken away at the end of the age.

Looking next to me, hoping to find a friend, Enoch had gone and I was left alone on what used to look like a beach. Resting in the goodness of God I had learned to trust in, I inhaled and exhaled deeply. I began to encourage myself, "God, You are amazing. I love You, I love You, I love You and I trust You deeply. Thank You for Your goodness and mercy. Whatever just happened and the reasons for it can only lead me closer to You."

I continued to praise Him and thank Him for a few more minutes. As I grew silent I heard someone and could very faintly make out what looked like a fuzzy, translucent figure in the distance. This astigmatism in the the spirit was no fun. As it began to get closer I felt a burning in my heart. It was Jesus. There was not a presence in the Universe that could make my heart burn like this. The burn was not painful; it was the burn of longing. When He got within ten feet of me I could see His eyes and took steps towards Him to give Him a hug. I went straight into His chest and I could feel His beard in my hair. After a long embrace he disengaged, looked me straight in the eyes and said, "Well done, now you can be lead by Love. Love will restore your vision and take you into places of clarity and knowledge that you could never have imagined."

Jesus was the embodiment of Love. My vision began to clear from hearing His voice and being around Him. I felt like a child just learning to walk, but His presence left nothing to be desired. As we were sitting together I addressed Him, "Hey. This is new. Can I ask you a question?"

"Certainly," He replied.

"Can you elaborate on the 'filter' thing?" I asked.

Jesus replied, "It is the difference between being in Heaven and looking down and being in the Earth and looking up. When you are in Heaven looking down, you can see all things and there is nothing standing in your way. When you are on Earth looking up, everything you receive is filtered through a filter that consists of multiple things. Some of those things are simple like your understanding of the Bible (not the Bible itself), others are more complex like the environment you grew up in. Much of your filter is in your DNA. Regardless of what the different parts of the filter are, you will never get a clear picture of who I am and who the Father is if you are learning it through a filter. If you desire to progress in relationship, the filter in your mind must be judged and you must walk away from everything you thought you understood. From here forward, if you did not learn it on the Heaven-side of the veil, it should be tossed. As you grow you may discover things that were similar to what you thought you understood, but you must throw away even the comparison. Begin again as a child."

Smiling and relieved I said, "That sounds like rest."

He replied with Love, "It's the best way."

Moving through my DNA as before and having the areas of the filter judged and healed was becoming easier. I also asked by Faith for the filter in my mind to be judged. This process took time and Jesus was with me the entire way. When I was finally finished I looked up and saw Him. He was my Savior. My Love. The One in whom all of my hope and joy originated and rested. Jesus Christ, the anointed King of Kings. The only door and gate to the Father. He who was slain before the foundation of the Earth. The God/Man whose life, death, burial, resurrection and ascension provided salvation for mankind. And, I was just meeting Him for the first time... again.

* black cloud: see final chapter "The Shoes" of Joseph's first book; "Chronicles of a Seer".

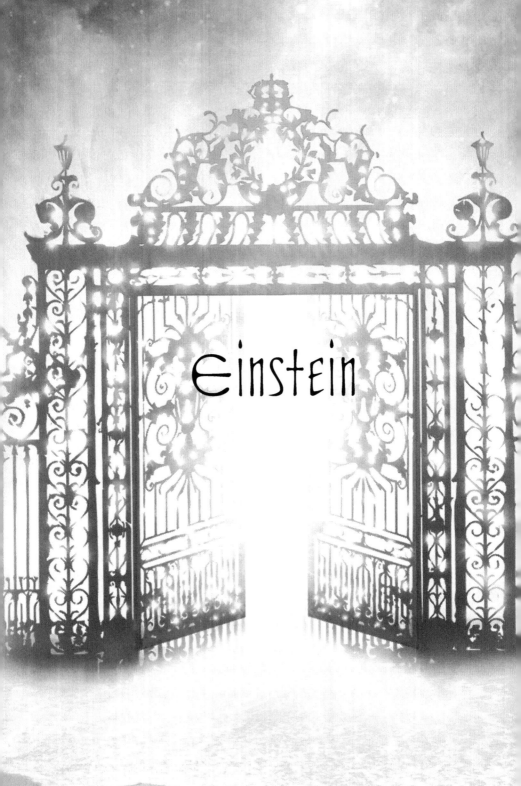

Einstein

Chapter 10

"Einstein"

Pathways for manifesting Heaven

Lying in bed (on Earth), I closed my eyes and began to engage Heaven before drifting off into never, never land. I have found it to be the most effective way to engage Heaven when my conscious mind checks out. As I began to engage, my conscious mind ceased and I fell asleep. At that exact same time I left my body, ascending through realms and dimensions and through creative darkness into a den with comfy chairs. Across from me, with one of the most gentle and loving looks I have ever seen, sat Albert Einstein. He had a funny smirk on his face but appeared to be the kind of man you would want to give a big hug. He was also surrounded and engulfed in knowledge that commanded awe. It was apparent that he was honored in Heaven. He was the embodiment of gentleness and knowledge. The Fear of the Lord was not far off either. Einstein began, "Hey Joseph, I want to talk to you about the pathways of the brain, the pathways of the Mind of Christ, the Seven Spirits of God and the Seat of Rest."

"That is a lot," I said.

Einstein continued, "It is a lot for you to retain if you use the pathways of your brain. It will be impossible if you try to process it in your brain instead of with Knowledge and Understanding in the mind of Christ, using the pathways created for your benefit and forward progress. It is actually a microscopically small amount of information you already know. It is time to begin to live from a higher place. What you are about to learn will be a building block."

"Great!" I responded.

Einstein was pleased, "It is such an honor to be involved in your generation and to be a part of releasing knowledge into the Earth."

Excited I said, "It's an honor to sit with you. My desire is to represent you well. Please continue with what you have."

Einstein continued, "These things I will mention together, make up the construct by which revelation comes from the spirit realm and manifest in your natural life. There are four layers we need to discuss. The first layer I want to speak about is the Seat of Rest. The Seat of Rest should be the beginning point for everyone. It is the place from which everything in your life is accessed and governed. The Seat of Rest is the starting point for inward omniscience, the Mind of Christ. If you are trying to access the Mind of Christ from anywhere but the Seat of Rest it will be very difficult. We will talk about that later. The omniscient, all-knowing part of the Mind of Christ is governed by the Seven Spirits of God. They are our tutors and they are the administrators of all knowledge. From the Seat of Rest, you can engage each one at a time or the full counsel of God regarding any matter. This is part of your inheritance as a Son and you have access to it all of the time. The amount you access will be a direct reflection of how much you enter into and remain in rest. From the Seat of Rest and the Seven Spirits of God there are pathways that lead down through the dimensions into your natural life. For the purposes of teaching you and showing you, I am going to separate them into the paths of the Mind of Christ and the paths of the brain. There are five paths but since I am separating the two it will seem as though there are ten. Pay attention.

"The pathways we will speak about are pathways, not gateways. Information can flow and you can approach them from either direction. Before we can speak about what the pathways are, you need to know what they look like. There are distinct pathways but all of them are lined and surrounded by something. When you travel from the Seat of Rest - to the Mind of Christ - to your brain - to your life, you are traveling dimensionally. These paths travel with no hindrance across those dimensions. The bridge by which information travels is an intertwining of things that are true, noble, just, pure, lovely, contain good news, contain virtue and things that are worthy of praise. These attributes also line the path. You can find them in Philippians 4:8 (NKJV paraphrased). Every pathway we are about to talk about travels surrounded by the above attributes and also operates across dimensions with multiple dimensions composed of the above. While these are ideas and truths that comprise a pathway, if you would like more information on them, they are also angelic beings. You just met 'Purity'. 'Lovely' is a being who loves over everything in Heaven that is exquisitely beautiful. You will learn much about yourself from the Father's perspective when you engage her.

"The first pathway I want to speak about is "Desire with Expectation". These are rooted and grounded in the Mind of Christ and are an access point for revelation and information to flow. Desire is the wanting for something to happen. Expectation is a strong belief something will happen. These two are anchored in the Mind of Christ as a pathway for revelation to travel down dimensionally into your brain. The connection point in your brain for these two is belief. The design is for you to, from rest, enter into the Mind of Christ (governed by the Seven Spirits) which will contain the Fullness of Knowledge and the Heart of God in a matter in order to gain the perspective and knowledge of Heaven. Once received, you allow the information to shape your desires and expectations which then travel down the path into your brain and mould your belief system. The belief system created will then begin to shape the world around you as well as your worldview. **The desire with expectation of Heaven received from rest in the Mind of Christ, governed by the testimony of the Seven Spirits, is how your entire belief system should be shaped.**

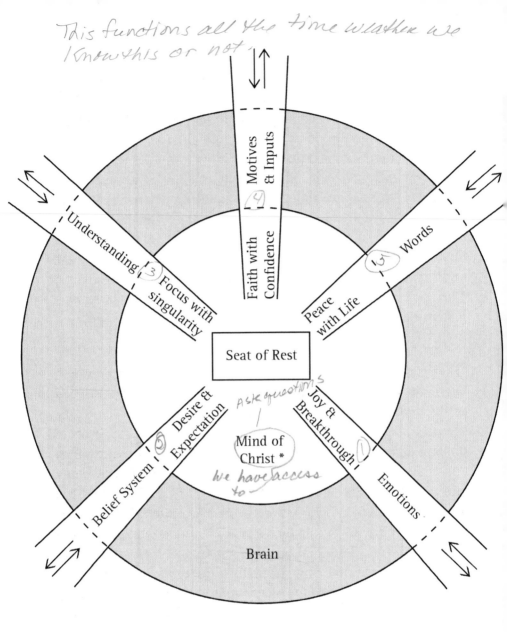

The paths are lined with the virtues described in Phillipians 4:8.
These virtues create an intra-dimensional bridge.

* The "Mind of Christ" contains: Access; Inward Omniscience;
Governance; Testimony of the Seven Spirits of God.

"The second pathway I want to speak about is "Joy and Breakthrough". Joy and Breakthrough also make up a path rooted in the Mind of Christ. Joy and Breakthrough always lead to each other. When Breakthrough comes, Joy comes. When Joy comes, so does Breakthrough. As you engage the Mind of Christ both of these will happen simultaneously in your mind and in your heart. They will travel together down the pathway into your brain. When they hit your brain they interact with your emotions causing immense Joy and Breakthrough in your emotions, releasing it into the world around you. Joy and Breakthrough in the Mind of Christ crosses over into your emotions in your brain. **The Joy and Breakthrough of Heaven received from rest in the Mind of Christ, governed by the testimony of the Seven Spirits, is how your emotions should be shaped.** *are traitors & gardians which are Are 7 spirit impowered by Holy Spirit*

"The third pathway I want to speak about is "Focus with Singularity". Focus and Singularity cannot exist apart. What you Focus on, you will connect to - but if your Focus is not Singular you will be distracted. It is an important path in the Mind of Christ, because it is an access point and because from Rest we keep our mind on things above. Our Singular Focus is "above." The Mind of Christ falls into this category. We must allow the Mind of Christ to shape our Singular Focus. The Singular Focus from the Mind of Christ flows down the path into our brain into our understanding. It is **with Singular Focus we receive complete clarity so that we may understand what is being communicated and said within the Mind of Christ from Rest. This ensures our understanding may be formed from the Mind of Christ and the Heart of the Father into our daily lives.**

"The fourth pathway I want to speak about is "Faith with Confidence". You have spoken before with many different people about Faith. Your level of confidence will be directly proportional to your Faith. These two are inseparable and lead to the part of your brain that has to do with motivation and intent of actions. From Rest our Faith and Confidence will shape the motives and intents of our hearts into physical actions that are birthed from the Mind of Christ.

"The last pathway I want to speak about is "Peace with Life". Peace with Life is inseparable from the Mind of Christ because it is a product of Rest. From Rest we engage the Mind of Christ and the revelation and information gathered travels down the path of Peace with Life into the part of our brain that deals with words. We then speak into our situation the Mind of Christ and the Heart of God. This concludes the paths of the Mind of Christ.

"There are a few things you should know. Information can travel both ways on these paths. Since you were born you were taught information comes from outside in, not inside out. Everyone at some point or another has used an external circumstance to try and figure out the Mind of Christ in a situation. What happens is we use external circumstances to formulate our belief system. Once that belief system is formulated we try and hold God to our desires and expectations which are based on a belief system that did not come from Him. They came from the wrong direction. This is how you go backwards on a pathway. It never works, but it is connected to the Mind of Christ, so sometimes what happens is that people get far enough up the pathway (even though it's the wrong direction) to actually see the Mind of Christ in the matter - which then puts them at Rest so they can engage it properly. The thing is, the entire time they are going the wrong direction, it is formulating a false belief system about who God is and how He operates. So the first thing that has to be dealt with once you enter Rest is all of the false junk you believe, because you have been operating in the wrong direction. This is what you did when you asked for all of the revelation you received about God while in the Earth (and not in Heaven) to be judged."

Once again I was speechless. There was nothing to ask. I felt honored beyond my wildest imagination. Einstein looked at me and said, "The honor is mine."

Einstein disappeared and I woke up.

Daniel

CHAPTER 11

"DANIEL"

CREATIVE POWER

Honored beyond my wildest expectation, I sat at home for eight days completely incapacitated and captivated by wonder and awe at the wisdom and expanse of The Father. It is truly immeasurable. After the eight days, as the weight began to lift, I decided I should get some fresh air. I live in Birmingham, Alabama and am a bit biased towards the beauty of my city. I decided to pick one of the beautiful walking trails and go for a stroll to see if I could come back to Earth a bit more. After walking for about an hour I found a picnic table and decided to sit down for a rest to look at the surrounding area and people-watch. It was and old-school wooden one, well-crafted and probably thirty years old. A thorough pressure wash and it would be good as new. I sat down and began to admire the beauty of creation around me. Admiring the beauty of nature around me caused me to begin to meditate inwardly on the beauty of Heaven. It is incomparable. Admiring the beauty of Heaven overtook my senses and I was instantly no longer at the picnic table and back on the beach. The only thing there to do, was laugh out loud. Joy swept over me like wind and the adventure was back on!

It did not appear as if anyone was coming, so I decided to walk towards the gate and see if it was a good idea to go through. There was no indication of anything so, knowing what I did about the gate, I decided to walk through again. With no delay I was outside the atmosphere of the Earth in the same dimensional place I met Ezekiel. Standing over the Earth, trying to take everything in, Daniel appeared next to me. He was accompanied with a Host of Heaven and they had purpose. When Daniel was in 'position', he turned to me and said, "There are certain scrolls that certain people will carry out. The scroll I am about to release is destined for all Sons and the time has come for you all to begin to step into it."

When he was finished Daniel reached inside of himself and pulled out a scroll. It was unsealed. He opened it and the top read "Creative Power." Daniel released the scroll into the Earth and all of Heaven shouted. When they were finished, Daniel and I went back through the gate to the beach.

Arriving on the beach, I took a deep breath, exhaled and turned to Daniel. Daniel smiled and said, "There were times on the Earth when a scroll like this one was only released once in a generation. In the days ahead there will be more scrolls released than in all of the generations combined. You are in a generation where everything that was sealed up in my day will begin to be released. The increase of knowledge, technology and the like, will be exponential. There was a mindset of 'it could not get better than this' that infiltrated the Church. As the knowledge is released, it will move to 'it is about to change for the better again.' Would you like to have a peek at a few of the things to be released?"

"Yes," I replied excitedly.

"I will show you like this," Daniel replied.

When Daniel finished the sentence a book appeared in his hand. The title was 'Astral Engineering'. I looked up at him astonished. He smiled and asked me to look again. Looking again the title changed to 'Creating Flora and Fauna'. Gasping, I looked at Daniel again and he asked me to look one more time. This time the title changed to 'Imaginative Creation, Building and Mending the World Around You.'

I was excited. Seeing my excitement, Daniel said, "This is a teaspoon-size sample of something as big as the Earth, and your generation will begin to explore it."

I was speechless and becoming accustomed to not having anything to say. I smiled at Daniel, thanked him and he disappeared.

Joseph the Carpenter

CHAPTER 12

"JOSEPH THE CARPENTER"

TREASURE OF DARKNESS

Wrecked beyond my wildest imagination, I sat on the beach in a puddle of awe, wonder and Fear of the Lord. I did not know whether to cry, laugh, levitate or enter into ecstatic joy. Whirlwinds of emotions engulfed me as I realized the Mercy and Grace that had come upon me during this journey and the Treasures hidden for me in Darkness, which had now been revealed in my day. Unsure of what to do next, I once again lay back into the sand, threw my arms over my head so that my hands could feel the sand and stared into the galaxies above, allowing myself to drift away in the arms of bliss. Once my hands felt the sand I was anchored in, there was no going back and I was set on enjoying and reflecting in this moment on the journey. For me, what just happened was beyond my wildest dreams and expectations. The manner in which the Father is able to show each of us love in a way so personal, yet so profound, is truly awe-inspiring. The mechanisms and relationships He has set us up to have, only add to the mystery of knowing Him intimately. For One so powerful, He loves really well.

As I lay basking I could feel the presence of gentleness beginning to approach me from behind. Assuming it was Jesus I turned to look. To my surprise and excitement it was not Jesus, but the man who stood in the role of His Earthly father. Joseph the Carpenter. He was the embodiment of gentleness. With great care he approached me smiling like someone who was in love with everything. Joseph embraced me like a Father and began to speak, "I am so excited to meet you, I have so much invested in your generation and the generations to come. I want to speak to you about what it was like to raise THE SON of God and what it looks like for you to raise sons of God and to Father them in the ways of Heaven."

Still a bit whacked from basking in glory, feeling like myself yet wanting to honor this man, I said the only (awkward) thing I could think of, "Um, YES."

Joseph, not expecting my comment, looked at me strangely and had a good laugh. Grabbing my hand he began to show me his life with Jesus on the Earth from a birds eye view, outside of time. I could see the excitement and fear of having the Magi visit at Jesus' birth. For Joseph the Carpenter the realization that his "son" was God came in layers, but the responsibility came all at one time. One day Joseph was a carpenter, the next he was entrusted with loving the most important man to walk the Earth and was having strange Magi visit and bring enormous wealth to him. Joseph did not have it all together and this was just the start.

After the scene with the many Magi, I was taken to Jesus' early childhood. Joseph loved Him so well. He was literally the light of Joseph's world and Joseph wanted everything for Jesus. There was nothing Joseph would not do for Him. Next, I went to the scene where Jesus was about twelve and he was sitting with the Rabbis. It was so different seeing it from Joseph's perspective. He was genuinely worried about his son. Jesus had been missing and Joseph loved Him. When Jesus was finally found, Joseph and Mary reacted as many parents would, "What are you doing? Why? Where have you been?"

Simply stated, they were afraid for The Son of God's life. They knew Him after the flesh. Jesus, at the time, was so wrapped in the Father's Heart that it did not make sense to Him why they would question where He was. Yet, even at twelve years old, Jesus was wise and humble enough to go with and obey parents who did not understand who He truly was and what He was doing. This was a day that marked Joseph, Mary and Jesus.

I was astounded with the things I was seeing. I never saw fathering a son from this perspective and how frustrating it must have been as a father for Joseph to have Jesus begin to walk in His calling. At this point, Joseph simply did not understand. It was also encouraging to realize while Jesus was without sin and his calling was Earth-shattering, it did not mean his closest relationships were easy. In fact, it made them harder. Very few understood His heart, which made love His only option. Jesus loved so well He actually began to father his Earthly father, Joseph. His life with His family was about the demonstration of love. The more He demonstrated love, the more His family learned of His true identity. He would do miracles in front of them that only they could see, not for the purpose of being understood, but for the purpose of demonstrating to them how His Father in Heaven loved. The amount of love and growth between Joseph and Jesus as father and son was paramount in Jesus' development and relationship with His Father in Heaven. The more Jesus loved Joseph, the more they both grew.

Exiting the encounter, Joseph smiled at me and said, "Come with me."

Walking up to the gate I knew this would be the last time. I admired the gate in all of its beauty and, with Joseph the Carpenter, stepped through to the other side. Upon arriving at the other side I was once again outside the atmosphere of the Earth. Standing a small distance away were Jesus and Joseph both in glorified form. It was so powerful I was glad I was not right next to them. Looking at them, I was in awe. Standing in front of me was Jesus of Nazareth and Joseph the Carpenter, His Earthly father! They were standing next to each other representing the embodiment of what it looks like to grow in relationship towards God together. Both fathers and both sons. They peered towards the Earth and locked hands. The instant they locked hands, an exchange began between them. Both began to grow; quickly they were much bigger than the Earth. As they grew, glory that looked like an electric substance exchanged between them in an almost constant stream. They were growing in size and also in stature together. This was a new realization of what it looked like to grow in favor with God and man. Finally, reaching out in perfect union towards the Earth, grasping it in their hands, Jesus and Joseph pulled it within themselves and looked towards me.

With my mouth gaping, I saw Jesus of Nazareth and Joseph the Carpenter, a God man and a Man in White, together becoming, representing and revealing what this journey was about; The Treasures of Fatherhood being revealed in the Earth. Humility, mourning, meekness, desire, mercy, heart purity, peacemaking and persecution (Matthew 5:3-10).

In unison together, Jesus and Joseph were declaring and enjoying the most coveted part of Fatherhood. Relationship with the son.

A Personal Note from the Author

I wanted to take some time and thank you. The journey through these two books has been long and glorious. Thank you. It may seem as though both books ended quite abruptly, they did. There is no amount of words that could change it. When the revelation stopped, so did I. The Treasures revealed in this book are the Treasures of Fatherhood, both from the perspective of Men in White Linen and also from the perspective of growing ourselves as fathers. In my opinion, to pattern our lives after the revelation and pattern laid out in the 'beatitudes' is time well spent. I had no idea how the book was going to fit together until I wrote the last three paragraphs. I was wrecked for days when I realized the whole book was about fathering. Reflecting on the book and the revelations presented together with the Men in White who presented them to me, has been the most honoring time in my life. Thanks again for sharing it with me.

This series has twelve (12) books. As of finishing this book, the only revelation I have of the next book is the title. It will be called "The Transcendent Life." I am excited and honored to share it with you as it is revealed in my life.

Cheers,

Joseph

About The Author

Joseph Sturgeon lives and works in Alabama. He loves spending time in heaven and recording these experiences in writing.

Otherwise you will find him enjoying the outdoors, being involved in the business world and traveling with friends.

More resources can be found at www.revelationrevealed.net

SeraphCreative

Heaven's Heart for Earth

Seraph Creative is a collective of artists, writers, theologians & illustrators who desire to see the body of Christ grow into full maturity, walking in their inheritance as Sons Of God on the Earth.

Sign up to our newsletter to know about the release of the next book in the series as well as other exciting releases.

Visit our website :

www.seraphcreative.org

Made in the USA
San Bernardino, CA
04 May 2017